Experiences of Hunger and Food Insecurity in College

Lisa Henry

Experiences of Hunger and Food Insecurity in College

palgrave
macmillan

Lisa Henry
University of North Texas
Denton, TX, USA

ISBN 978-3-030-31817-8   ISBN 978-3-030-31818-5   (eBook)
https://doi.org/10.1007/978-3-030-31818-5

This Palgrave Pivot imprint is published by the registered company Springer Nature Switzerland AG.
The registered company address is: Gewerbestrasse 11, 6330 Cham, Switzerland

In memory of Rodney Mitchell

ACKNOWLEDGMENTS

First, I would like to thank the students at the University of North Texas (UNT) for their trust and sharing of their deeply personal stories. This research has been humbling and has deepened my understanding of what students in my classes and around campus may be going through in their lives while attending college. I would also like to thank the UNT Dean of Students, particularly Maureen "Moe" McGuinness and Rodney Mitchell (in memorandum), for their partnership on this research project. Their support and dedication to the students at UNT is remarkable, and their collaboration with the well-being of students in mind has facilitated this work that will hopefully lead to more solutions. The data collection was funded by a UNT Scholarly and Creative Activity Award through the College of Liberal Arts and Social Sciences. I thank my research team of graduate and undergraduate students in the Department of Anthropology— Emma Carnes, Jena Chakour, Ana Belen Conrado, Beth Holland, Bridget Landis, Kelly McFarland, Skye O'Neill, Andie Semlow, Sarah Stutts, and Ashley Thomas. I thank the UNT Department of Anthropology for their support with a graduate research assistant, Kelly McFarland, who helped with coding, analysis, and the report to the Dean of Students. I also want to thank Caitlin Griffith for her assistance with the references and her unending support, professionally and personally. Finally, I want to thank my family—Doug, Riley, Will, Tory, JoJo, and Junior—for their endless support, encouragement, sacrifices, and love.

CONTENTS

ABOUT THE AUTHOR

Lisa Henry is Professor of Anthropology at the University of North Texas. She holds a PhD from Southern Methodist University. As an applied medical anthropologist, her research interests include food insecurity, biomedicine and healthcare delivery, anthropology in public health, globalization and health, and indigenous healing systems. Her regional specializations are the U.S. and the Pacific Islands. She is the Past-President of the National Association for the Practice of Anthropology (NAPA).

LIST OF FIGURES

LIST OF TABLES

CHAPTER 1

Introduction

Abstract The introduction chapter sets the stage for the context of this research topic and the manuscript. I introduce the concept of food insecurity in the U.S. by presenting USDA definitions and current statistics in the broader U.S. population. Next, I discuss the growing awareness and attention to food insecurity among college students by highlighting the increasing research on the prevalence and experience of food insecurity in college across the U.S. Next, I discuss the research project, research design, and methodology of my qualitative, ethnographic research at the University of North Texas (UNT). I highlight this project's contribution to the literature on food insecurity among college students. I interviewed 92 students who were clients of the UNT Food Pantry. This is the largest qualitative study to be published to date, and it captures student perspectives on the meaning and experience of food insecurity.

Keywords Food insecurity • Food insecurity in college • Qualitative • Ethnography

> *Food is the last priority. I'd rather sleep on a bed and have a roof over my head than eat.*

© The Author(s) 2020
L. Henry, *Experiences of Hunger and Food Insecurity in College*,
https://doi.org/10.1007/978-3-030-31818-5_1

At the time of this research, Cassandra was a 20-year-old African-American sophomore at the University of North Texas. As a freshman, she lived in the dorm, had a meal plan, and *ate like it was the holidays with almost every meal*. Like many college students, in the summer after her freshman year, she moved into an apartment with two friends who shared the rent. The following fall semester she took four classes and worked *as much as she could*. The hours she worked varied from 15 to 30 hours per week, mostly determined by the scheduling manager at work, but also by her class schedule. Her job paid minimum wage, and as Cassandra explained, *it's hard to find a high paying job that also has the flexibility to work with my class schedule. A lot of college students end up changing jobs every semester.* Cassandra noted, *I pay for everything—the rent, the bills. I go to class. I go to work. I try to study. Sometimes, when I don't work enough, I don't have money for food. At the same time, I can't work all the time and go to class. I have to choose.*

Cassandra was a federal Pell Grant recipient and also received some loan money. Her mom helped financially as much as she is able. During her freshman year, Cassandra noted that it was easy to manage all the expenses because food and housing were wrapped up together. When she first moved into an apartment, all of the different bills and expenses were overwhelming to organize and pay between the three roommates. She thought she would have enough money with her job but quickly realized that her finances varied month to month. Her older sister tried to help out with expenses by giving her money from time to time, but it was not consistent. Cassandra often did not have enough money to pay all of her bills and eat consistently. She depended on the UNT Food Pantry to help fill the gap.

Cassandra's story is one of many that resonates with college students across the U.S. Although the notion of the hungry college student is not new, the issue is receiving increasing national attention including in the popular press, among researchers, and university administrators.

1.1   FOOD INSECURITY IN THE U.S.

The United States Department of Agriculture (USDA) defines food security as access for all household members to "enough food for an active, healthy life" at all times. It includes easily accessible nutritionally adequate and safe foods, as well as the ability to secure foods in socially acceptable

Table 1.1 USDA food security categories (USDA 2018a)

Food secure	High food security	Households had no problems, or anxiety about, consistently accessing adequate food.
	Marginal food security	Households had problems at times, or anxiety about, accessing adequate food, but the quality, variety, and quantity of their food intake were not substantially reduced.
Food insecure	Low food security	Households reduce the quality, variety, and desirability of their diets, but the quantity of food intake and normal eating partners were not substantially disrupted.
	Very low food security	At times during the year, eating patterns of one or more household members were disrupted and food intake reduced because the household lacked money and other resources for food.

ways (i.e. not stealing, scavenging, or accessing emergency food sources such as food pantries). Conversely, the USDA defines food *insecurity* as having limited or uncertain access to healthy, nutritionally adequate, and safe food or the limited ability to acquire food in socially acceptable ways. Other characteristics of food insecurity include reduced calorie intake, lack of variety in diet, hunger without eating, and reduced weight due to lack of calories (USDA 2018a). Table 1.1 shows the continuum of food insecurity status and the economic and social contexts that define each. Hunger, an individual physiological condition, is too difficult to measure according to the USDA, but the very low food security category is associated with hunger. Households that fall into that category report eating less than they felt they should, skipping meals, and/or reducing meal sizes (USDA 2018a). See Himmelgreen and Romero-Daza (2010) for a thorough discussion on the implications for eliminating the word "hunger" from U.S. food policy.

According to the most recent USDA food security survey, the estimated percentage of U.S. households that were food insecure in 2017 was 11.8 percent (15 million households). This figure is down from 12.3 percent in 2016 and includes both low food security and very low food security. When analyzed further, the estimated percentage of U.S. households that were very low food secure in 2017 was 4.5 percent (5.8 million), down from 4.9 percent in 2016 (Coleman-Jensen et al. 2018).

Importantly, the prevalence of food insecurity varies by household type. Table 1.2 shows that certain household types have food insecurity rates above the national average:

Table 1.2 Food insecurity by household characteristics (USDA 2018b)

National average	11.8%
Households with children under age 6	16.4%
Household with children headed by a single woman	30.3%
Households with children headed by a single man	19.7%
Women living alone	13.9%
Men living alone	13.4%
Black, non-Hispanic households	21.8%
Hispanic households	18.0%
Low-income households (below 185% of the poverty threshold)	30.8%

Between 2015 and 2017, Texas experienced household food insecurity rates higher than the national average and ranked 11th highest overall with 14 percent of households experiencing food insecurity (USDA 2018b).

1.2   Food Insecurity Among College Students

There has been an increase in the national attention to food insecurity and hunger on U.S. college campuses. According to Feeding America (2018), one in ten adults they serve are college students. Of the households they serve, 31 percent choose between paying for education and food every year. Prevalence studies on a single university campus report a range of 14–59 percent of students being food insecure at some point during their college career (Chaparro et al. 2009; Hughes et al. 2011; Gaines et al. 2014; Patton-López et al. 2014; Maroto et al. 2015; El Zein et al. 2018; Willis 2019; Weaver et al. 2019). More recent cross-sectional, multi-university studies report a range of 35–50 percent, with an average of 44 percent of students being food insecure while attending college (Bruening et al. 2017; Global Food Initiative 2017; Broton and Goldrick-Rab 2018; Broton et al. 2018; Crutchfield and Maguire 2018; Martinez et al. 2018; Nazmi et al. 2018; Goldrick-Rab et al. 2019a; Goldrick-Rab et al. 2019b; Goldrick-Rab et al. 2019c). In April 2019, the Hope Center for College, Community, and Justice published the largest nationwide assessment of basic needs security among college students. In this fourth year of the nationwide survey, they collected data from 86,000 college students from 123 two-year and four-year colleges in 24 states. In breaking down the data, 48 percent of students from two-year colleges and 41 percent of students from four-year colleges experienced food insecurity in the previous 30 days. Nearly half of all students reported not being able to afford balanced meals (Goldrick-Rab et al. 2019a). What is clear from these studies is that college students are disproportionally food insecure when compared to the national average of 11.8 percent.

The scholarly research on multiple aspects of food insecurity among college students is rapidly expanding, and the U.S. government is also starting to take note. In December 2018, the U.S. Government Accountability Office published a report to Congress that reviewed food insecurity among college students. The report examines "(1) what is known about the extent of food insecurity among college students and their use of SNAP; (2) how selected colleges are addressing student food insecurity; and (3) the extent to which federal programs assist students experiencing food insecurity" (GAO 2018, X).

Food insecurity among college students is not entirely a new phenomenon. Baby Boomers and Generation Xers have their own stories of pinching pennies and eating peanut butter and jelly sandwiches for weeks to make ends meet. The contemporary rise in prevalence is related to a number of issues. Generations ago, many high school graduates went on to manufacturing jobs or other workforce positions that did not require a college degree. Today, a college degree is seen as an available next step (Goldrick-Rab 2016) and the major key to a successful career and financial security (Hughes et al. 2011; Hout 2012; Carnevale et al. 2014; Ma et al. 2016). According to the Center for Law and Social Policy (CLASP), the demographic profile of undergraduate college students is shifting. They are older, first-generation, low-income, working, more diverse, and have more family obligations to balance. Approximately 40 percent are over age 25, 51 percent are independent, 42 percent are students of color, 51 percent are low-income, 66 percent work at least part-time, 26 percent are parents, and 15 percent are single parents (CLASP 2015; Nellum 2015; U.S. Department of Education 2015; GAO 2018). In short, many college students are already considered vulnerable populations.

According to Sara Goldrick-Rab in *Paying the Price: College Costs, Financial Aid and the Betrayal of the American Dream* (2016), low-income students often do not have enough financial resources to cover the cost of college. The average estimated price in 2018–2019 of a public four-year university with in-state tuition, on-campus room and board, plus supplies and transportation, was $25,890. The cost for a public two-year, in-district commuter was $17,930 (College Board 2019). The federal Pell Grant, which is based on financial need, is worth approximately $6000, not nearly enough to cover the cost. Students also apply for additional financial aid, taking out large loans to cover the difference. As Henry (2017) notes, most students who are under 24 years of age are considered dependent (in regard to federal financial aid eligibility) and must have their parents' financial information on the Free Application for Federal Student Aid (FAFSA) form. Yet, many students are under 24 years of age and financially independent, but do not qualify for an exception to the parent requirement (see https://studentaid.ed.gov/sa/fafsa/info-graphicaccessible). For these students, if parents refuse to fill out the financial information, their financial burden increases significantly because they are not eligible for federal financial aid.

Students try to make up their financial deficits by working. The 2019 Hope Center for College, Community, and Justice's national report shows that 68 percent of students who experience food insecurity work at least part-time (Goldrick-Rab et al. 2019a). The research discussed in this manuscript shows that 72 percent of participants work at least part-time while in college. The employment status of food insecure students is particularly important as it relates to their eligibility for federal food programs (such as SNAP). Similar to Cassandra, students struggle to make ends meet with low-paying jobs. Not only do these jobs have varying hours per week, but students also need jobs that can work with their ever-changing schedules from semester to semester.

1.3   A Deep Dive: Ethnographic Research on Food Insecurity at UNT

This manuscript is the result of a research project at the University of North Texas (UNT) with the Dean of Students department. UNT is a large, public research university in north Texas located roughly 40 miles north of both Dallas and Fort Worth. It has a total enrollment of just over 39,000 and offers 105 bachelor's, 88 master's, and 37 doctoral degree programs. The student body is 52 percent minority and 48 percent White. UNT was named to the 2019–2020 Military Friendly Schools list and has been listed as one of America's 100 Best College Buys for 23 consecutive years. About 75 percent of UNT students receive financial aid and scholarships (www.unt.edu).

The UNT Dean of Students is a department within the Division of Student Affairs, a large division that ensures the holistic development of students. Broadly, the Division of Student Affairs has 30 departments that focus on Wellbeing and Safety, Career and Leadership, Student Life, and Engagement and Support. The Dean of Students serves as an advocate for all students and is dedicated to helping them achieve their academic and personal goals. Based on their work with students who struggle financially, who are sometimes housing insecure, and who need referrals to city resources for emergency food services, the Dean of Students Office opened a food pantry in January 2015.[1] The food pantry serves any current UNT student in need, and there are no additional criteria for access. The Dean of Students has protocols to ensure student confidentiality and dignity throughout their food pantry experience. Students may request a meeting with the Dean of Students staff to address specific difficulties they are having, and additional campus and community resources are offered when necessary. In addition to the main food pantry at the University Union, there are smaller food pantries at two satellite campuses—Discovery Park and UNT's New College at Frisco. The vision for the UNT Food Pantry is for the UNT community to partner with the pantry in order to take a collective approach to ensure that no UNT student lacks the fuel and security to succeed in achieving their academic and personal goals. Many departments, including the UNT Community Garden, have partnered with the food pantry to fill its shelves (Dean of Students 2018).

I first partnered with the Dean of Students to conduct a research project on student food insecurity in August 2014, five months before the food pantry opened. Because of the increased attention to food insecurity among college students in the popular press, I wanted to conduct an exploratory pilot project with my graduate Ethnographic and Qualitative Methods class. Being a qualitative methods class, I explained to the Dean of Students that we wanted to conduct a qualitative study, rather than a quantitative prevalence study. Our goal was to identify students who self-identified as food insecure and explore the meaning and experience of food insecurity while in college—a deep dive into their stories. The Dean of Students was eager to partner and noted that she did not need a prevalence study at the time because she already knew food insecurity was a problem at UNT. The department had already committed to opening a food pantry. Since the UNT Food Pantry was not open yet, the research population for this pilot study was students who self-identified as food insecure or hungry. The sample size was 27 students (see Henry 2017 for details on this project).

Two years later, in February 2017, the Dean of Students and I partnered again to conduct a larger study with student clients of the UNT Food Pantry, which had 1754 visits since its opening two years earlier. Our goal was three-fold:

1. To re-examine our research questions with a larger sample,
2. To investigate unexpected themes from the pilot study, and
3. To evaluate the food pantry.

Our specific research goals were:

1. To investigate the meaning of food insecurity as perceived by college students,
2. To investigate the experience of food insecurity as college students and in childhood,
3. To investigate the barriers to accessing food assistance programs (on campus and off campus),
4. To investigate eating habits, nutrition, and coping strategies,
5. To investigate the association of physical and mental health with food insecurity,
6. To investigate academic sacrifices and motivations for staying in college,
7. To evaluate the UNT Food Pantry, and
8. To investigate local solutions to food insecurity in addition to the food pantry.

1.3.1   Methodology

Funded through a UNT Scholarly and Creative Activity Award, I recruited seven graduate students and three undergraduate students for my research team. Some team members worked on the project for course credit; others volunteered their time for research experience. All research assistants were trained in ethics and interviewing.

The research population was students, past or current, who were clients of the UNT Food Pantry. Recruitment consisted of direct e-mails, class announcements, flyers, and announcements on Blackboard Learn. The Dean of Students sent recruitment e-mails to all previous clients of the food pantry. Food pantry clients were offered $25 as a participation incentive for a 60–90 qualitative interview. Those interested in participating contacted Lisa Henry, who coordinated the interview schedule with the research team. The research team consented each participant in person. The study protocol was approved by the Institutional Review Board at the University of North Texas.

Interviews included open-ended questions on household composition, financial situation, how students define food insecurity, student stories of food insecurity, the timing of food insecurity, childhood experiences with food insecurity, experience with off-campus social services, conversations about food insecurity, physical health, mental health, nutrition, dietary and medical needs related to food insecurity, academic success, academic motivation, coping strategies, eating habits, solutions (on-campus and off-campus solutions), and a section on the evaluation of the food pantry. We opted for scaled questions to measure students' mean scores of food pantry overall experience, confidentiality, helpfulness, and the adequacy of the amount of food. Each of these scaled questions was followed up with an open-ended question asking students to explain their rating.

Interviews also included the U.S. Department of Agriculture's (USDA) 10-question food security module (USDA 2017). We chose to administer this standardized food security module to establish a comparison measure across college food insecurity studies. Although we did not conduct a prevalence study, measuring food insecurity categories with our population helps to understand and compare experiences among students with similar food insecurity categories across studies. We chose to use 12 months as a timeframe because college students' schedules, housing, and employment change frequently. Their food insecurity status changes frequently. For freshman, we verified that their experiences with food insecurity occurred after the start of college and not solely prior to college.

The research team collected 92 valid interviews from February 2017 to July 2017. This equaled 100 hours and 42 minutes of recorded interview time, which transcribed into 3320 pages of text. Transcripts were uploaded to MaxQDA software and coded using 140 codes and subcodes. Codes were generated by topics covered in the interview, as well as themes that emerged inductively. Using MaxQDA, each code was analyzed for patterns in the data. Furthermore, code reports were pulled using demographic variables and other codes as filters to compare subsets of students. For example, students who experienced childhood food insecurity were separated from those who did not experience it in order to analyze their coping strategies while food insecure during college.

This project is the largest qualitative study on food insecurity among college students to date. For additional qualitative studies, see Henry (2017), Meza et al. (2018), Allen and Alleman (2019), Allen (2019), Dhillon et al. (2019), and Hattangadi et al. (2019). This study captures the students' voices, their perspectives, their experiences, the meanings they give to food insecurity, and their everyday practices of being food insecure and hungry while trying to finish their degrees. Chilton and Booth (2007) note that lived experiences of individuals often disappear in the food insecurity discourse, which makes these stories important to capture and share (see also Himmelgreen and Romero-Daza 2010). Mulligan and Brunson (2017) discuss the importance of collecting the richness of stories. People's stories highlight the meaning and experiences of their lives. They give research participants time to elaborate on the important context of their perspectives and behaviors that might otherwise be blind spots in research. Finally, Mulligan and Brunson highlight that, through collecting stories to "saturation," rather than to generalization, this allows qualitative researchers to consider all narratives as truth, not just the dominant narrative.

1.4   Overview of Book

This book is organized into five main chapters that cover the major themes of this research—experience and meaning, stigma and shame, physical/mental health and nutrition, and academic success and motivation.

In Chap. 2, I detail the major research demographics, explore the self-reflective meaning of food insecurity from the perspective of college students experiencing it, detail the seven main profiles of experience, and tell the students' stories of food insecurity while attending college. This chapter also emphasizes the overlapping factors that contribute to food insecurity in college. Next, I discuss the different coping strategies utilized by students. Finally, I examine students' experience with food insecurity as children and how those experiences have shaped their experiences in college.

Chapter 3 is a major focal point of my research. I begin with a discussion on Goffman's notion of shame and then move into a review of literature on the concept of shame as failure. Next, I provide an overview of the food insecurity and shame literature among college students. Since there are few studies that touch on stigma and shame in college, I expand this review to include the general population. Though no questions were asked directly about stigma or shame in the UNT research, it emerged as a predominant theme. I highlight the five sub-themes students discussed about stigma and shame. Next, I discuss college students' willingness to talk about their food insecurity with others. Finally, I highlight the potential to destigmatize stigma through increased awareness by university engagement with all students in a broad conversation about food insecurity and hunger on campus.

Chapter 4 begins with a literature review on the negative health outcomes associated with food insecurity and poor dietary habits in the general population. I briefly review the literature on K-12 students before detailing the expanding research on college students. Next, I discuss the research at UNT and detail the physical consequences of food insecurity as described by students. The next section discusses the association of mental health issues with hunger and poor nutrition, starting with the general literature, then among college students, and next among UNT students. Finally, I end the chapter with a discussion about how nutrition fits into their stories about food insecurity and their physical and mental health.

Chapter 5 begins with a literature review on food insecurity and academic success among K-12 students, followed by a discussion of the expanding research on college students. Interview participants were asked if food insecurity has impacted their student success or performance in a course. This chapter shows the grit needed to be academically successful despite food insecurity. I discuss specific academic sacrifices in order to have more money for food, followed by a discussion of any activities, in class or extra-curricular, that were avoided because of issues with food insecurity. The final section discusses what motivates students to stay in college while they are food insecure.

Chapter 6 begins with a discussion on the importance of evaluating programs designed to reduce food insecurity in order to understand and measure their success. Next, I discuss the rise in food pantries across the nation, followed by a discussion on the evaluation of the UNT Food Pantry. Pantry clients were asked to evaluate, on a scale of 1–10 (10 being the highest), several aspects of their experience, including topics related to overall experience, confidentiality, helpfulness of the pantry, opinions about the amount of food, how the pantry helped, pantry items most wanted, and opinions about the layout of the pantry and the hours. Next, I discuss other local solutions suggested by UNT Food Pantry clients. Finally, I briefly discuss various programs that are occurring across the nation, including a discussion of current legislation designed to bolster attention to food security among college students.

A few notes about the writing of this manuscript: I use "students," "participants," and "food pantry clients" interchangeably. When referring to students, I am discussing the students who participated in this research project, all of whom were clients of UNT Food Pantry. I use the term "we" to refer to the research design partnership and the data collection team. I use the term "I" when referring to any analysis or writing. I use "college" and "university" interchangeably. Finally, for each participant who is quoted, I highlight a few demographic characteristics that I felt would give the reader a picture of who is speaking. Generally, I focus on age, ethnicity, and year in school, but also include if the participant was married, lived on campus, or was an international student since those characteristics were not the majority. I highlight these characteristics the first time a participant is mentioned in each chapter, even if they were mentioned in a previous chapter.

NOTE

1. It is beyond the scope of this manuscript to discuss all the resources available to UNT students. However, because broader solutions to financial hardship will be discussed in Chap. 6, it is important to point out that prior to establishing the UNT Food Pantry, the Dean of Students already had an emergency fund for catastrophic situations and distributed cafeteria food vouchers to students in crisis on a case-by-case basis. Additionally, the Student Money Management Center already established an emergency assistance loan program.

REFERENCES

Allen, Alejandro C. 2019. *Study Hard, Eat Less: Exploring Food Insecurity Among College Students*. Master's Thesis, Texas State University, San Marcos, TX.

Allen, Cara Cliburn, and Nathan F. Alleman. 2019. A Private Struggle at a Private Institution: Effects of Student Hunger on Social and Academic Experiences. *Journal of College Student Development* 60 (1): 52–69. https://doi.org/10.1353/csd.2019.0003.

Broton, Katharine, and Sara Goldrick-Rab. 2018. Going Without: An Exploration of Food and Housing Insecurity Among Undergraduates. *Educational Researcher* 47 (2): 121–133. https://doi.org/10.3102/0013189x17741303.

Broton, Katharine, Kari Weaver, and Minhtuyen Mai. 2018. Hunger in Higher Education: Experiences and Correlates of Food Insecurity among Wisconsin Undergraduates from Low-Income Families. *Social Sciences* 7 (10): 179. https://doi.org/10.3390/socsci7100179.

Bruening, Meg, Katy Argo, Devon Payne-Sturges, and Melissa N. Laska. 2017. The Struggle Is Real: A Systematic Review of Food Insecurity on Postsecondary

Education Campuses. *Journal of the Academy of Nutrition and Dietetics* 117 (11): 1767–1791. https://doi.org/10.1016/j.jand.2017.05.022.

Carnevale, Anthony, Stephen Rose, and Ban Cheah. 2014. *The College Payoff: Education, Occupations, Lifetime Earnings.* Center on Education and the Workforce. https://1gyhoq479ufd3yna29x7ubjn-wpengine.netdna-ssl.com/wp-content/uploads/collegepayoff-completed.pdf. Accessed 10 Apr 2019.

Center for Law and Social Policy (CLASP). 2015. *Yesterday's Nontraditional Student is Today's Traditional Student.* Report. http://www.clasp.org/resources-and-publications/publication-1/CPES-Nontraditionalstudents-pdf.pdf. Accessed 7 Mar 2017.

Chaparro, M. Pia, Sahar S. Zaghloul, Peter Holck, and Joannie Dobbs. 2009. Food Insecurity Prevalence among College Students at the University of Hawai'i at Mānoa. *Public Health Nutrition* 12 (11): 2097–2103. https://doi.org/10.1017/s1368980009990735.

Chilton, Mariana, and Sue Booth. 2007. Hunger of the Body and Hunger of the Mind: African American Women's Perceptions of Food Insecurity, Health and Violence. *Journal of Nutrition Education and Behavior* 39 (3): 116–125. https://doi.org/10.1016/j.jneb.2006.11.005.

Coleman-Jensen, Alisha, Matthew P. Rabbitt, Christian A. Gregory, and Anita Singh. 2018. *Household Food Security in the United States in 2017.* Report No. 256. U.S. Department of Agriculture, Economic Research Service.

College Board. 2019. *Average Estimated Undergraduate Budgets, 2018–19. Average Estimated Undergraduate Budgets, 2018–19.* Trends in Higher Education. https://trends.collegeboard.org/college-pricing/figures-tables/average-estimated-undergraduate-budgets-2018-19. Accessed 7 June 2019.

Crutchfield, Rashida, and Jennifer Maguire. 2018. *Study of Student Basic Needs,* January. https://www2.calstate.edu/impact-of-the-csu/student-success/basic-needs-initiative/Documents/BasicNeedsStudy_phaseII_withAccessibilityComments.pdf. Accessed 17 May 2019.

Dean of Students. 2018. University of North Texas. deanofstudents.unt.edu/resources/food-pantry. Accessed 6 Aug 2018.

Dhillon, Jaapna, L. Karina Diaz Rios, Kaitlyn Aldaz, Natalie De La Cruz, Emily Vu, Syed Asad Asghar, Quintin Kuse, and Rudy Ortiz. 2019. We Don't Have a Lot of Healthy Options: Food Environment Perceptions of First-Year, Minority College Students Attending a Food Desert Campus. *Nutrients* 11 (4): 816. https://doi.org/10.3390/nu11040816.

El Zein, Aseel, Anne Mathews, Lisa House, and Karla Shelnutt. 2018. Why Are Hungry College Students Not Seeking Help? Predictors of and Barriers to Using an On-Campus Food Pantry. *Nutrients* 10 (9): 1163. https://doi.org/10.3390/nu10091163.

Feeding America. 2018. *Learn More About Hunger in America.* http://www.feedingamerica.org/research/hunger-in-america/facts-and-faces/. Accessed 17 May 2019.

Gaines, Alisha, Clifford A. Robb, Linda L. Knol, and Stephanie Sickler. 2014. Examining the Role of Financial Factors, Resources and Skills in Predicting Food Security Status among College Students. *International Journal of Consumer Studies* 38 (4): 374–384. https://doi.org/10.1111/ijcs.12110.

Global Food Initiative: Food and Housing Security at the University of California. 2017. Report. University of California, December. https://www.ucop.edu/global-food-initiative/_files/food-housing-security.pdf. Accessed 2 Apr 2019.

Goldrick-Rab, Sara. 2016. *Paying the Price: College Costs, Financial Aid, and the Betrayal of the American Dream.* Chicago, IL: University of Chicago Press.

Goldrick-Rab, Sara, Christine Baker-Smith, Vanessa Coca, Elizabeth Looker, and Tiffani Williams. 2019a. *College and University Basic Needs Insecurity: A National #RealCollege Survey Report.* Report, April. https://hope4college.com/wp-content/uploads/2019/04/HOPE_realcollege_National_report_digital.pdf. Accessed 18 May 2019.

Goldrick-Rab, Sara, Vanessa Coca, Christine Baker-Smith, and Elizabeth Looker. 2019b. *City University of New York #RealCollege Survey.* Report, March. https://hope4college.com/wp-content/uploads/2019/03/HOPE_realcollege_CUNY_report_final_webversion.pdf. Accessed 18 May 2019.

———. 2019c. *California Community Colleges #RealCollege Survey.* Report, March. https://hope4college.com/wp-content/uploads/2019/03/HOPE_realcollege_CUNY_report_final_webversion.pdf. Accessed 18 May 2019.

Government Accountability Office (GAO). 2018. *Better Information Could Help Eligible College Students Access Federal Food Assistance Benefits.* Report. U.S. Government Accountability Office, December. https://www.gao.gov/assets/700/696254.pdf. Accessed 18 May 2019.

Hattangadi, Nayantara, Ellen Vogel, Linda Carroll, and Pierre Côté. 2019. "Everybody I Know Is Always Hungry…But Nobody Asks Why": University Students, Food Insecurity and Mental Health. *Sustainability* 11 (6): 1571. https://doi.org/10.3390/su11061571.

Henry, Lisa. 2017. Understanding Food Insecurity Among College Students: Experience, Motivation, and Local Solutions. *Annals of Anthropological Practice* 41 (1): 6–19. https://doi.org/10.1111/napa.12108.

Himmelgreen, David, and Nancy Romero-Daza. 2010. Eliminating "Hunger" in the U.S.: Changes in Policy Regarding the Measurement of Food Security. *Food and Foodways* 18: 96–113. https://doi.org/10.1080/07409711003708611.

Hout, Michael. 2012. Social and Economic Returns to College Education in the United States. *Annual Review of Sociology* 38 (1): 379–400. https://doi.org/10.1146/annurev.soc.012809.102503.

Hughes, Roger, Irene Serebryanikova, Katherine Donaldson, and Michael Leveritt. 2011. Student Food Insecurity: The Skeleton in the University Closet. *Nutrition & Dietetics* 68 (1): 27–32. https://doi.org/10.1111/j.1747-0080.2010.01496.x.

Ma, Jennifer, Matea Pender, and Meredith Welch. 2016. *Education Pay 2016: The Benefits of Higher Education for Individuals and Society*. Report. New York: College Board. https://trends.collegeboard.org/sites/default/files/education-pays-2016-full-report.pdf. Accessed 15 Apr 2019.

Maroto, Maya E., Anastasia Snelling, and Henry Linck. 2015. Food Insecurity among Community College Students: Prevalence and Association with Grade Point Average. *Community College Journal of Research and Practice* 39 (6): 515–526. https://doi.org/10.1080/10668926.2013.850758.

Martinez, Suzanna M., Karen Webb, Edward A. Frongillo, and Lorrene D. Ritchie. 2018. Food Insecurity in California's Public University System: What Are the Risk Factors? *Journal of Hunger & Environmental Nutrition* 13 (1): 1–18. https://doi.org/10.1080/19320248.2017.1374901.

Meza, Anthony, Emily Altman, Suzanna Martinez, and Cindy W. Leung. 2018. "It's a Feeling That One Is Not Worth Food": A Qualitative Study Exploring the Psychosocial Experience and Academic Consequences of Food Insecurity Among College Students. *Journal of the Academy of Nutrition and Dietetics*, December 12. https://doi.org/10.1016/j.jand.2018.09.006.

Mulligan, Jessica, and Emily Brunson. 2017. The "Anecdote" Insult, or Why Health Policy Needs Stories. *Medical Anthropology Quarterly*, March 7. http://medanthroquarterly.org/2017/03/07/the-anecdote-insult-or-why-health-policy-needs-stories/#. Accessed 24 May 2019.

Nazmi, Aydin, Suzanna Martinez, Ajani Byrd, Derrick Robinson, Stephanie Bianco, Jennifer Maguire, Rashida M. Crutchfield, Kelly Condron, and Lorrene Ritchie. 2018. A Systematic Review of Food Insecurity among US Students in Higher Education. *Journal of Hunger & Environmental Nutrition*. 1–16, June 22. https://doi.org/10.1080/19320248.2018.1484316.

Nellum, Christopher. 2015. Fighting Food Insecurity on Campus. *Higher Education Today*. http://www.higheredtoday.org. Accessed 1 Mar 2016.

Patton-López, Megan M., Daniel F. López-Cevallos, Doris I. Cancel-Tirado, and Leticia Vazquez. 2014. Prevalence and Correlates of Food Insecurity among Students Attending a Midsize Rural University in Oregon. *Journal of Nutrition Education and Behavior* 46 (3): 209–214. https://doi.org/10.1016/j.jneb.2013.10.007.

U.S. Department of Education. 2015. *Demographic and Enrollment Characteristics of Nontraditional Undergraduates: 2011–2012*. Report. Washington, DC. https://nces.ed.gov/pubs2015/2015025.pdf. Accessed 24 May 2019.

US Department of Agriculture (USDA) Economic Research Service. 2017. *Food Security in the U.S. Survey Tools*. https://www.ers.usda.gov/topics/food-nutrition-assistance/food-security-in-the-us/survey-tools/#household. Accessed 20 Sep 2018.

———. 2018a. *Food Security in the U.S. Measurement.* https://www.ers.usda.gov/topics/food-nutrition-assistance/food-security-in-the-us/measurement/. Accessed 8 Sep 2018.

———. 2018b. *Food Security in the U.S. Key Statistics & Graphics.* https://www.ers.usda.gov/topics/food-nutrition-assistance/food-security-in-the-us/key-statistics-graphics/. Accessed 8 Sep 2018.

Weaver, Robert R., Nicole A. Vaugh, Sean P. Hendricks, Penny E. McPherson-Myers, Qian Jia, Shari L. Willis, and Kevin P. Rescigo. 2019. University Student Food Insecurity and Academic Performance. *Journal of American College Health*, May 7. https://doi.org/10.1080/07448481.2019.1600522.

Willis, Don E. 2019. Feeding the Student Body: Unequal Food Insecurity among College Students. *American Journal of Health Education* 50 (3): 167–175. https://doi.org/10.1080/19325037.2019.1590261.

CHAPTER 2

Meaning and Experience of Food Insecurity

Abstract This chapter begins with a discussion on the research sample demographics because *who* the students are is wrapped tightly with their experiences of food insecurity. Next, I highlight the self-reflective meaning of food insecurity from the perspective of college students experiencing it. The majority of students focus on the emotional aspect of food insecurity or worrying about their next meal. The next section describes the seven non-mutually exclusive profiles of food insecurity experiences in college. This section also emphasizes the overlapping factors that contribute to food insecurity in college. Next, I discuss the different coping strategies utilized by students. The participants described 276 non-mutually exclusive coping strategies that fell into eight broad themes. Finally, I examine students' experience with food insecurity as children and how those experiences have shaped their experiences in college. Fifty-eight percent of participants reported experience with childhood food insecurity.

Keywords Food insecurity • Demographics • Experiences • Coping • Childhood

© The Author(s) 2020   17
L. Henry, *Experiences of Hunger and Food Insecurity in College*,
https://doi.org/10.1007/978-3-030-31818-5_2

2.1   DEMOGRAPHICS OF STUDY PARTICIPANTS

This chapter begins with a discussion on the research sample demographics because *who* the students are is wrapped tightly with their experiences of food insecurity. Previous research highlights that underserved and underrepresented groups in college may be at greater risk of financial and food insecurity (Cady 2014; Patton-López et al. 2014; Payne-Sturges et al. 2018; Martinez et al. 2018; Freudenberg et al. 2011; Broton et al. 2018; Nazmi et al. 2018; Goldrick-Rab et al. 2019). The overrepresentation of African-American students in the UNT research sample (see below; also Henry 2017) supports a significant pattern noted in the literature. African-American students are significantly more likely to be food insecure than non-African-American students (Freudenberg et al. 2011; Maroto et al. 2015; Morris et al. 2016; Twill et al. 2016; Payne-Sturges et al. 2018; Goldrick-Rab et al. 2019; Weaver et al. 2019). Interestingly, research shows that students who identify as Hispanic or Latinx also experience higher rates of food insecurity (Maroto et al. 2015; Miles et al. 2017; Forman et al. 2018; Martinez et al. 2018; Weaver et al. 2019). Yet, the UNT sample population of self-identifying Hispanic or Latinx students was slightly under representative of the UNT Hispanic student population (see below). Other underserved and underrepresented groups that have been identified as at risk for food insecurity include low-income (Patton-López et al. 2014; Goldrick-Rab et al. 2019), student-parents, LGBTQ students, former foster youth (Goldrick-Rab et al. 2019), international students (El Zein et al. 2018), first-generation college students (Forman et al. 2018), and those who experienced food insecurity as children (Martinez et al. 2018; Broton et al. 2018). Additionally, several studies show that students who live off campus are at greater risk for food insecurity than those who live on campus (Calvez et al. 2016; El Zein et al. 2018; Broton et al. 2018).

The UNT research sample was drawn through convenience. Food pantry clients who saw the recruitment e-mails and announcements came forward to volunteer for participation. The sample is not random, and I do not claim that it represents all food insecure students at UNT. However, there are stories in this demographic data from those who volunteered to talk with us about their experiences. We collected data on gender, age, year in school, location of residence, household composition, and financial situation (work, financial aid, financial assistance from others, financial responsibility for others, and credit card use).

Fig. 2.1   Age range

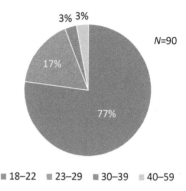

N=90

■ 18–22   ■ 23–29   ■ 30–39   ▨ 40–59

Fig. 2.2   Gender

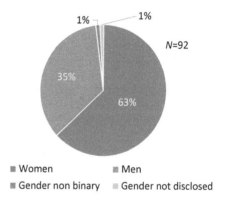

N=92

■ Women   ▨ Men
■ Gender non binary   ▨ Gender not disclosed

The sample is 77 percent 18–22 years old, 63 percent female, 94 percent single, 59 percent upper-class students, and 40 percent African-American (Figs. 2.1, 2.2, 2.3, 2.4, and 2.5).

Table 2.1 highlights the comparison between the research participants and the overall UNT demographic data. The research participants are slightly more female (participants 63%, UNT 53%) and upper class (participants 59%, UNT 50%) than the overall UNT student body. Comparative differences show in categories of age and ethnicity. The research participants are 77 percent 18- to 22-year-olds, whereas the UNT student body is 48 percent. The research participants are 40 percent African-American, whereas the UNT student body is 14 percent. The participants are also 17 percent Hispanic, whereas the UNT student body is 23 percent.

Fig. 2.3   Marital status

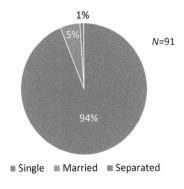

Fig. 2.4   Ethnicity (not mutually exclusive)

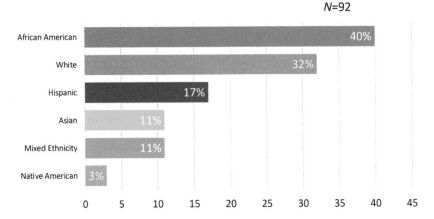

The majority of participants lived in apartments (68%), but 25 percent lived in dormitories on the UNT campus. It is vital for university administrators to understand that even with meal plans, students find it difficult to get all of the nutrition they need (see profile 4). Only seven percent of the research sample lived in single-family housing. These students did not live at home with their families and did not participate in everyday household economies of the households where they grew up. The majority lived near campus with roommates (81%) and were not financially responsible for others (85%). Over half of the participants were (self-reported) food insecure as children (58%) (Figs. 2.6, 2.7, and 2.8).

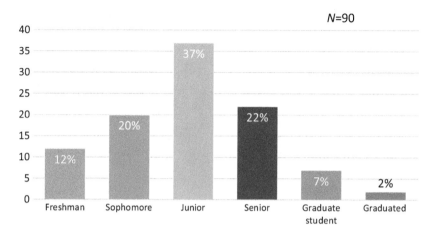

Fig. 2.5   Year in college

Table 2.1   Sample vs. UNT demographics (UNT Fact Sheet 2017)

	Sample frequency	Sample percentage	UNT percentage
Women	58	63	53
Men	32	35	47
Gender non-binary	1	1	–
Gender not-disclosed	1	1	–
18–22 years old	69	77	48
23–49 years old	21	23	52
Single	85	94	–
Married	5	5	–
Separated	1	1	–
African-American	37	40	14
White	29	32	47
Hispanic	16	17	23
Mixed	10	11	–
Asian	10	11	7
Native American	3	3	2
Freshman	11	12	15
Sophomore	18	20	18
Junior	33	37	22
Senior	20	22	28
Graduate students	6	7	17
Graduated	2	2	–

Fig. 2.6 Living
situation

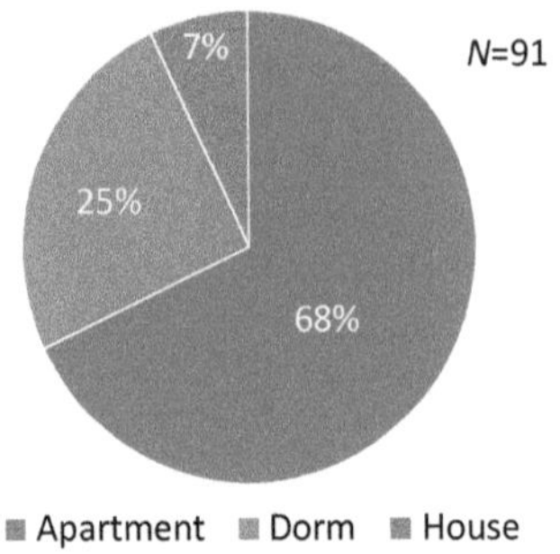

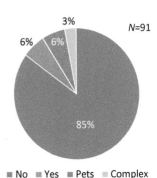

Fig. 2.7 Financially
responsible for others

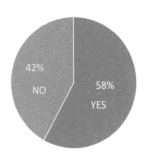

Fig. 2.8 Food insecure
as children

2.2   FINANCIAL SITUATION

As noted in Chap. 1, food insecure students work to try to overcome their financial deficits. Weaver et al. (2019) note that college students work either part-time or full-time while taking classes and still accumulate substantial debt over their college careers (see also DeRuy 2015; Friedman 2018). Also noted in Chap. 1, the 2019 Hope Center for College,

Community, and Justice's national report shows that 68 percent of students who experience food insecurity work at least part-time (Goldrick-Rab et al. 2019). The report also shows that of working students, basic needs (housing and food) insecure students are more likely to work and work longer hours than students who are basic needs secure (see also Freudenberg et al. 2011; Patton-López et al. 2014).

Asking college students if their work is more complicated than a simple yes/no answer gives insight into the financial struggles of food insecure students. The majority (59%) of UNT food insecure students said that they worked while food insecure (mostly part-time work). The 28 percent who said that they did not work cited various reasons for their current employment status. Some depended on GI Bill benefits and military stipends. They wanted to focus on finishing school. Others worked in the summer, took too many credit hours to work, or were looking for a job. Others had academic circumstances that prevented them from working. One student mentioned that she was in a theatrical show and spent her time at rehearsals. Another student said that she was student teaching and was required to focus solely on this requirement. Another 13 percent of students could not be classified as working or not working because of the fluidity of their work situation. Ryan, a 19-year-old African-American who lived on campus, captured their experiences well with his story:

> I had a great job over the summer, but then I came to school and I couldn't figure out how to keep my schedule with my classes. It just wouldn't work out. I didn't want to quit that job. It was a great job. But the timing didn't work out. So, I got a different job, but it had less hours. That wasn't enough so I found a second job where the hours were better but the pay was less than the first job. I messed up juggling two jobs and school, and now I don't work anywhere. I had to stop at both of those jobs.

Students struggle to keep well-paying flexible jobs that fit with their ever-changing class schedule (see also Allen 2019) (Fig. 2.9).

The overwhelming majority of students reported receiving financial aid (96%) in the form of loans (78%), grants (75%), and scholarships (54%). The majority also received some form of financial help from others (65%). Of those who receive financial help from others, only 27 percent stated that they had steady help either with tuition, bills, or some form of steady stipend per month, even a small stipend. A greater 38 percent stated that financial help came sporadically and only when there was a specific need. Some students asked their family for money to cover rent, a specific bill, or even groceries. Other students noted that family would periodically give

Fig. 2.9 Working
while food insecure

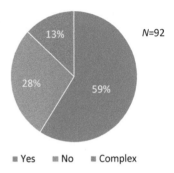

N=92

■ Yes   ■ No   ■ Complex

them cash to cover whatever they needed. Only 15 percent of those who received some financial support from others receive it from people other than their parents, including grandparents, uncles, aunts, siblings, and significant others. Tish is a 20-year-old African-American senior who explained: *I don't really receive that much from my mom. It's hard for her to help me out. My older sister helps me out also. She helps me out when she can because it's hard being a college student, not getting paid well, and trying to keep everything in balance. She understands.* Twenty-eight percent of students stated that they receive no support at all. Finally, nine percent of students stated that they could ask for financial assistance from family, but it was an absolute last resort because it made them feel guilty and uncomfortable (Figs. 2.10 and 2.11).

The majority of students (59%) did not use credit cards to buy food when they did not have enough money. They reported fear and trepidation about credit cards, though most recognized the benefits of building credit. Of those who did use credit cards to purchase food (37%), they articulated a strong understanding of the credit card use and payment. Most had balances on their cards and could afford to pay only the minimum payment due. They noted that food, especially restaurant food, contributed to their credit card balances. They also noted needing the credit card periodically for unexpected large expenses. Aditya, a 22-year-old South Asian international graduate student, noted: *I had to pay for a $550 expense this month so I didn't have enough money to buy groceries. I had to use my credit card only for this month. But usually I use the credit card only to gain some credit history. That's the main reason I use the credit card.* A few students discussed using multiple credit cards and some expressed remorse for overusing them (Fig. 2.12).

Fig. 2.10 Receives financial aid

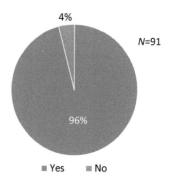

Fig. 2.11 Receives financial help from others

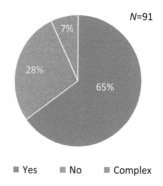

Fig. 2.12 Uses credit card for food

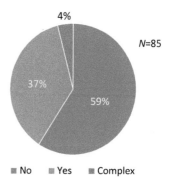

2.3   The Meaning of Food Insecurity

As noted in Chap. 1, we chose to administer the U.S. Department of Agriculture's (USDA) 10-question food security module (USDA 2017). We chose to administer this standardized food security module to establish a comparison measure across college food insecurity studies. Our sample of 92 clients of the UNT Food Pantry indicates that 67 percent are very low food secure (with hunger) and another 18 percent are low food secure. Collectively, 85 percent of our sample is low food secure. Students who have experienced childhood food insecurity, have self-identified mental health issues, and have experienced decreased self-identified student success experience low food security more than those who do not fall into those categories ($p < .05$ for each) (Fig. 2.13).

The USDA defines food insecurity as having limited or uncertain access to healthy, nutritionally adequate and safe food or the limited ability to acquire food in socially acceptable ways (USDA 2018). When students at UNT talked about food insecurity, they mostly talked about worry and fear (43%). Food insecurity for them meant not knowing if they would have enough money to eat and not knowing where or how they would get their next meal. Students were constantly worrying and thinking about not having enough food, and according to the participants, this psychological stress impacted their mental health and academic success (see Chaps. 4 and 5; see also Meza et al. 2018).

At the time of the research, Cameron was a very low food insecure UNT student who chose not to share demographic information other than her gender. She shared her story of being homeless about 90 percent of her life. When she and her mom moved from California to Texas, they

Fig. 2.13 USDA food security categories

did not have anywhere to go, so they mostly stayed late at restaurants and 24-hour stores like Wal-Mart, and slept in cars or stayed with people they met. They scraped by any way they could, including going to soup kitchens and food pantries, but they never stayed in a shelter. When Cameron started UNT, she had scholarships and grants to cover her tuition but worked to pay her other bills. She lived with her boyfriend, and they worked together to pay the rent, even after he lost his job. Cameron did not have a car so she depended on him for rides to and from work. But when they broke up, she found herself on her own. Her mom had moved to Georgia. Her dad lived in California. The rest of her family was in Mississippi. She ended up losing her job because she could not get to work. She lost her SNAP benefits because she did not have a job. She did reach out to her parents, but they had their own financial issues at the time. She remembers saying to herself: *oh Lord, what am I gonna do?* That was the moment she started going to the UNT Food Pantry. Months later, she got a shared apartment and claimed it was the first time in a long time that she had a steady roof over her head. When asked what food insecurity meant to her, she noted: *I would say basically not knowing where your next meal's coming from, or just being scared because you're hungry. And you don't want to ask for help, but then you kind of need help, so, I would say that's probably a good definition of food insecurity.*

Linda, a 21-year-old Hispanic/White senior, shared a similar meaning: *I guess, [food insecurity] is just this knowledge that you don't have food available to you or maybe you worry about it a lot. It's something that you worry about or you feel unsatisfied with the amount that you have or what you have.* Erika is a 19-year-old White sophomore who lived on campus. She added:

> *I think if you are not certain that you are going to have a meal that will fill you up and be nutritious. If you are not able to get those things and are worried about it, you're food insecure. If you are buying Ramen for every meal, I think that counts because that's not giving you what you need. A lot of people I think construe it as you have no money for food ever. I don't think that's what it is. I think it's when you are able to buy food one day this week but then the rest of time you either did not eat or you ate something really bad for you because it was all you could afford.*

Though worry and fear is the strongest theme, there are several other reflections on the meaning of food insecurity. Students discussed being hungry, not having enough food to eat, and not caring about what type of food they were eating as long as it was food (27%). Students also described food insecurity as not getting adequate nutrition because they ate *crappy, processed, and fast food* (23%). Brianna, a married 23-year-old African-American senior, described growing up with food insecurity:

> *We would have peanut butter and jelly sandwiches, or old school honey sandwiches. Yeah, a lot of sandwiches. So that's when I think of food insecurity. That's what I see. I see no vegetables. I see no fruit. I see not having access to healthier food. I consider fast food a food insecurity, because you don't have enough money to get decent food. So, you get fast food and it gets you full, but it's not good for your body.*

Other students defined food insecurity as rationing food and money to make food stretch (22%). Sixteen percent of food pantry clients tied the meaning of food insecurity to being embarrassed about not having enough to eat and stigma inducing. Finally, many students (15%) defined food insecurity in relation to resources or lack of resources. They noted limited social capital and no backup plan, meaning they had no money, no friends/family to help out, and were not sure where to find food.

2.4   PROFILES OF FOOD INSECURITY EXPERIENCES IN COLLEGE

The strength of qualitative research is the opportunity to deep dig into the realities of student food insecurity experiences. Clients of the UNT Food Pantry were asked a series of open-ended questions about their experiences and allowed to talk as long as they needed. The first question broadly asked them to talk about their experiences with hunger and food insecurity while in college. Follow-up questions asked them to discuss when they first became food insecure as students, their perceptions of their food insecurity when they first went to the food pantry, and their perceptions of their current food insecurity status. Seven non-mutually exclusive profiles of food insecurity experiences in college emerged inductively from the data. In this section, I highlight these profiles and let the students tell their stories.

1. Tipping points: the most dominant profile is students who experienced tipping points during the semester (40%). These students were previously financially stable, but once a significant life event

occurred, their finances became unstable. Examples of tipping points are changes in living situations, reduction in work, car accidents, medical crises, parents stopping financial assistance, and so forth. These students could identify a moment or reason for their financial instability. In a 2014 study, Gaines et al. found that 42 percent of participants had experienced some form of shock (or tipping point), which was associated with increased food insecurity risk. College students, particularly low-income marginal college students, do not often have emergency funds to mitigate spontaneous financial hardships (Gaines et al. 2014). Juan, a 25-year-old Hispanic international student in his second year, explained:

I haven't had a job in like over six months. I was in a car accident last year. So, I can't really get a car because they won't finance one without a job. And I can't get a job because I don't have a car and I can't get anywhere. That's the situation I've been in. I've been getting help from friends and family, but I've gone to the food pantry three times because I don't have much money to eat.

Linda's story is similar to Cassandra's story:

My first couple of years here I was in the dorms and I got a full ride scholarship for my academics. That was pretty much the only reason I was able to come to school in the first place. And that was my only way of funding anything. I didn't have anything coming in from outside. I didn't have any parent income or my own personal income at the time. So, I was dependent on the meal plan and the occasional money that I get from babysitting or something like that. I had a Monday through Friday meal plan though, so weekends were kind of up to me. Sometimes I wouldn't have a whole lot to make it through the weekend, but I would just eat whatever I had or borrow from my roommate or something like that. That's how I maintained it, and once I got out of the dorms and moved into my apartment, it was even harder. I managed to get a job on campus, and that primarily paid for my rent. But the rest of it, maybe 5 percent of it, went towards food. I haven't gone days where I specifically went to sleep hungry in that sense, but I have struggled just to have food in general. The food pantry has helped a lot.

2. Lack of finances and budgeting issues: 19 percent of students talked about not being able to make it financially no matter how hard they tried. They worked as much as they could, but did not have enough

to cover all of their expenses. Their explanations for their circumstances were limited. One stated that her semester credit hours were too high to allow for enough time to work. Two students noted that they were on full scholarship, but the scholarship was not enough to live on. They did not want to work so much that their grades (and scholarship) were impacted, but they did not have enough money to cover their expenses. John, an 18-year-old African-American freshman who lived on campus, explained:

I want a job, but I can't really afford to get one, mainly because I have a lot of my plate, like research papers and college and all. And then also, before college, obviously there was hunger problems at home, which is why I'm not angry being hungry because I'm used to it. So, I'm going to be hungry in college too. That's cool.

Brad is a 25-year-old White junior who moved out of his parents' house when 18 years old. He was homeless, lived out of a car, slept in parking lots, ate free food at grocery stores, and hustled for other money. Two years prior to this interview, he quit his full-time job to come back to school. He had a part-time job that paid $400 per month, but his rent was $700 per month. His student loans helped, but he often scrambled or hustled in order to get food. In the past five months he had eaten nothing but canned foods, and he admitted to wanting the $25 participation incentive for this project so that he could buy bacon and eggs for the first time in months.

3. <u>Short-term food insecurity</u>: some students (17%) needed the food pantry at specific times to make it over a financial hurdle. Most of these times were at the beginning of the semester before their financial aid arrived, at the end of the semester when their financial aid ran out, or between paychecks. One student told a story of his supervisor making a mistake on his timesheet resulting in less income temporarily. Lynn, a 19-year-old Asian/White sophomore, explained:

This semester I didn't have a job and my FAFSA took a long time. There was a processing issue so there was a time when I had no money. All of my money went to rent. My grandparents and my parents helped as much as they could, but I really didn't have a whole lot so I decided to go ahead and try the food pantry.

Gabby, a 22-year-old African-American senior who lived on campus, added: *I've had that week to where you know rent was more important than me getting actual food…so…I didn't eat much until the next paycheck.*

4. Living in dorms with limited meal plans: 16 percent of students reported living in dorms with meal plans that provided unlimited swipes in the cafeterias Monday through Friday, but did not have access to the cafeteria on the weekends. Even the cheapest five-day meal plan includes FLEX. FLEX is flexible spending that can be used in the eateries and stores in the student union. Students reported spending FLEX money much more quickly than expected, particularly their first year. Several of them noted: *The union restaurants are expensive.* Once their FLEX money was gone, they had no money for food on the weekends. One campus resident, who did not share demographic information, stated: *I wish I could eat better on weekends, but there's not a lot of healthy options that are cheap.* Bruening et al. (2016) also show that low-income first-year students living in dormitories often choose a lower-priced meal plan and are forced to skip meals. Dubick et al. (2016) report that 43 percent of students with meal plans in a national survey reported food insecurity. Madeleine, an 18-year-old African-American freshman, explained:

Usually on the weekends I eat maybe like a meal a day and some snacks if I have them. Sometimes I don't eat, but it's not horrible. I usually have some-one I know who will have a little bit of food. I don't have a lot of money. I guess I should have gotten more FLEX, but I thought it would be a waste of money. I didn't spend it frivolously, but I usually used it on the weekends… until I ran out. I wish I could eat better on the weekends.

5. Transportation issues: transportation issues limited mobility to work, school, and food stores among 14 percent of students. These students noted that it was very difficult to find a good job within walking distance. There is a city bus system, but students found the routes limited and time-consuming. They also stated that walking to and from the grocery store took too much time. The closest grocery store to the university is two miles, but food insecure students lived all over the suburban town. They were more likely to depend on a friend to drive them, but then became reliant on the friend's

schedule. Many of these students found it easier to eat conveniently located fast food and used the campus food pantry while they were on campus (see Hager et al. 2017 for a recent study on the impact of food swamps and food deserts). Dhillon et al. (2019) also show that food insecure college students make food choices based on convenience due to lack of time, lack of transportation, and academic demands.

6. <u>Supplement groceries</u>: A few students (9%) talked about the food pantry as a useful supplement to their groceries. They downplayed their need to use the food pantry and yet half were very low insecure with hunger and five were food insecure as children. Possibly these students had a limited need, but it is also possible that they did not want to emphasize or focus on their food needs. Adam, a 24-year-old White senior, noted:

> *Sometimes it's nice to have stuff provided for you, you know? And not have to worry about when you need to go shopping and how much you're going to spend. It's nice to have some help.*

Monica is a 22-year-old African-American senior who talked about going to the UNT Food Pantry about once every three months. She described her needs as some days being worse than others and sometimes just needing a little bit of food to supplement her groceries. She also actively sought out free food events on and around campus.

> *First of all, I don't have a job right now. I haven't had a job probably since the beginning of the semester. It was a seasonal job. I can't get food stamps because you have to work 20 hours a week if you're a student, at least 20 hours. So that kinda sucks. I mean, I have food, but some days are worse than others, you know. And I would come to the food pantry probably like once every 3 months to get canned goods. Stuff like that allows for a little bit extra. And then I'll go to the grocery store and get like meat and stuff that I can't get at the food pantry.*

7. <u>International students</u>: We interviewed five international students (5%) whose stories were similar. They had no family in the U.S.; they were restricted to on-campus jobs, and they did not have cars. They were used to eating home-cooked meals in their home countries,

but noted that they did not know how to cook American food (see also El Zein et al. 2017; Hattangadi et al. 2019). They also knew it would be cheaper to cook at home and bring food to campus, but cited too much pressure of homework and class to spend time with meal preparation. Aditya, a 24-year-old South Asian international master's student, told his story:

I am an international student. So, when I came here it was very hard to deal with a new situation because in India, we use to have food everywhere, like on roads or small shops. It was all very cheap. It is very hard for me to be in a new situation where all things cost a lot of money. So, I came here and didn't have a job right away. I searched and searched. For first one month or one and a half months it was very hard for me to cook the food. I never cooked food back in India. Boys never cook food in India. At least I didn't do it. We don't even know how to cook the food or how to get vegetables and the quantity of all the things. I tried the cafeteria, but it is too costly. So, my roommates and I had to learn to cook the food. We learned what vegetables we should get and what meat we should get.

The stories of all 92 participants fit into one or more of these seven profiles. They are stories of students struggling to balance classes, studying, work, commuting, social engagements, and their expenses. The next section will explore more about their specific experiences with coping strategies.

2.5   Coping Strategies

The U.S. has formal federally funded safety-net programs such as the Supplemental Nutrition Assistance Program (SNAP), the Special Supplemental Nutrition Program for *Women, Infants, and Children* (WIC), subsidized school lunch programs, and subsidized housing. Despite the high rates of students experiencing food insecurity in college, the use of federally funded safety-net programs among college students is low. Goldrick-Rab et al. (2019) report that only 20 percent of students with food insecurity receive SNAP benefits and 57 percent utilize some form of public assistance program (see also GAO 2018). Broton and Goldrick-Rab (2018) report that 41 percent of very low food insecure students have used SNAP or other food-related public assistance. Although 54 percent of UNT students have had some experience with federal social services at some point in their lives, services such as SNAP benefits and subsidized housing were not discussed as coping strategies among students (see Chap. 3 for discussion on social services and stigma).

Previous research shows that for individuals and households in the general public, in addition to using federal programs, they also use informal coping strategies such as cooking at home (McIntyre et al. 2003), stretching food, substituting cheaper ingredients, reduced meal size, reduced meal frequencies, eating expired or nearly expired food, and cooking in bulk (Radimer 1990; Kempson et al. 2003; De Marco et al. 2009). Research on university students shows similar coping strategies (Lee et al. 2018; McArthur et al. 2018).

Lee et al. (2018) conducted a literature review on English-speaking developed countries and found a pattern of university students employing coping strategies related to food, income, and social support. Food-related coping strategies include purchasing cheap, processed food, eating smaller portions to stretch food, eating less healthy meals, skipping meals, food sharing with roommates and friends, and drinking water to suppress hunger (Hanna 2014; Henry 2017; Watson et al. 2017; Miles et al. 2017; McArthur et al. 2018). Income-related coping strategies include using a credit card to buy food, working more hours, strategically paying bills at various deadlines, and selling possessions (including plasma) (Gaines et al. 2014; Watson et al. 2017; Miles et al. 2017; Henry 2017; McArthur et al. 2018). Farahbakhsh et al. (2017) and Hanbazaza et al. (2017) also note that students apply for additional loans to secure more financial resources. Social support-related coping strategies include borrowing food/money from their social network, using food pantries, and attending free food events on campus (Gaines et al. 2014; Watson et al. 2017; Henry 2017; Miles et al. 2017; Allen 2019).

2.5.1   *At the University of North Texas*

At UNT, the university food pantry has played a major role in coping with food insecurity since it opened in early 2015. However, students discussed a wide variety of coping strategies, and several strong patterns emerged from our discussions. We asked participants to describe a typical day during periods of food insecurity and then asked: "How do you cope?" "What are your strategies?"

Ninety-two participants described 276 non-mutually exclusive coping strategies. These responses fell into eight broad themes (Table 2.2).

Table 2.2   Food insecurity coping strategies

Broad coping strategy themes	
Strategies to gain access to food to reduce hunger	60%
Behaviors to stave off hunger without eating	34%
Specific grocery buying habits	26%
Physical activities to distract from hunger	25%
Strategies to increase money for food	16%
Call on support network	16%
Redirecting thoughts and changing mindset	15%
Childhood influences on coping strategies	9%

Strategies to gain access to food to reduce hunger were by far the most common coping strategies (60%). Participants discussed making meals that lasted multiple days, planning menus and meal preparation, looking for free food events on campus, eating food on hand so it was not wasted, working in establishments that provide free meals for shifts worked, buying food in bulk and cooking, buying store brand items instead of name brand items, using coupons, and eating as much food as possible at the university cafeterias. Lois, a 21-year-old African-American senior, explained:

> *Um, well I do have food in my pantry so I'll look at what I have in my pantry and try to make something. I had like a pound of beans so I just throw it in a crock pot, and eat beans, then I had beans for like the past week. I guess like just peeking at my pantry and seeing what I have, and if I need to get something from the grocery store, then I'll go get something from the grocery store to make it for the most part.*

Alexis is a 20-year-old African-American sophomore who discussed shopping:

> *I guess grocery-wise, get something that lasts long. Get non-perishable foods. Get something in bulk. I know Winco's a really great place. You can get a pound of pancake mix for $.70 versus just getting a box that has less than a pound of pancake mix. I also use coupons.*

Participants also talked about behaviors to stave off hunger without eating (34%). Out of all the coping strategies mentioned, the single most used strategy to cope with food insecurity was sleeping. Twenty-five percent of all participants took naps or slept more if they got too hungry. Chloe, a 20-year-old multiracial junior, admitted to taking over-the-counter sleeping pills to pass out:

> *I have a very bad habit of self-sacrifice because I would rather have a place to sleep than eat. I just went days without eating, and I ended up putting myself in a very bad, like, health situation. I would just stop eating and lost a lot of weight. I would literally just like, you know, just take a sleeping pill and knock myself out. I would just go to sleep and pretty much sleep through the hunger. You know, just basically keep going until I passed out.*

Other behaviors related to staving off hunger without eating included drinking water (17%) (the 3rd overall most frequent strategy), drinking other beverages (such as coffee, soda, tea, milk), and chewing gum.

Another broad theme for coping with food insecurity was engaging in activities to distract themselves from hunger (25%). Students admitted trying to forget about their hunger by studying, playing video games, going outside, hanging out, working more, and even playing sports, although they noted that playing sports also takes calories they cannot afford to lose. Lynn shared her story:

> *Well, sometimes I'll just try to drink water. I'll try not to think about the food too much because I have a big appetite. I'm a hungry girl. And I found distraction, like hanging out with friends, is very good whenever you're sitting alone a lot of the time. I mean, even if you're not food insecure, boredom can lead to eating, whether you need it or not. And so, I just try to be entertained and try to focus on other things. Depending on how bad it is, I'll just like nap (laughs). Honestly, a lot of the time just trying not to think about it.*

Other strategies included attempts to secure more money (such as selling plasma), calling on their support network, redirecting their thoughts or changing their mindset, and leaning on their childhood experiences with food insecurity for support. Trinity, a 20-year-old African-American sophomore, spoke about changing her mindset as a strategy:

> *I know that God provides for everything, like for everything, but I'm like dang, I don't even have nothin'. I have nothing. I know every day when I wake up that I'm not gonna starve today. I'm gonna be able to go to school, and it's basically like, I'm gonna wake up and put a smile on my face. I'm not trippin about anything. I look at the brighter side of it instead of being like, 'oh my gosh, what am I going to eat, oh!'*

Destiny, a 21-year-old African-American junior, added: *I don't know. I think I just adopted the mindset of like…you're not gonna die, Destiny, if you have only two dollars in your bank account. I don't know, I had to realize like money is not everything.*

2.6   Impact of Childhood Food Insecurity

Capturing childhood experiences of food insecurity contributes to understanding how those experiences may shape students' experiences in college and how they cope. One student who never experienced childhood food insecurity stated: *I never had a problem with hunger growing up. That's why going to the food pantry is so shameful for me right now. I'm on my own in college because my dad lost his job.* Another student who did experience childhood food insecurity stated: *I have a very bad habit of sacrificing eating to pay my bills. Housing is more important to me. Being able to go to school is more important than my health. I have always pushed [hunger] aside.*

The literature highlights the adverse effects of childhood hunger, such as reduced ability to manage stress and weaker future job performance. A policy report by Feeding America notes that childhood food insecurity creates a workforce pool that is less competitive because adults are not well-prepared physically, mentally, emotionally, or socially to perform effectively in the contemporary workforce (Cook and Jeng 2009). Childhood food insecurity has also been linked with depression, anxiety, stress, negative cognitive development, and suicidal ideation, particularly in young adults (Alaimo et al. 2001; McLaughlin et al. 2012; Hanson and Olson 2012; Pickett et al. 2015).

Fifty-eight percent of participants reported experiences with childhood food insecurity. When asked what impact that experience has had on their college experience, students discussed (1) coping strategies (different from the aggregated analysis above); (2) proactive strategies to reduce food insecurity; (3) their relationship to food; and (4) budgeting. Coping strategies included pushing hunger aside, knowing how to cope, having an easy transition because of their past experience, and understanding needs versus wants. Corbin, a 19-year-old African-American freshman who lived on campus, said: *So, you know, it's just having that mindset that you've been in worse situations. It's like 'oh okay, this is not that bad.' It's helped me maintain like…I've been through a lot. You can make it.* Molly is a 19-year-old White freshman who lived on campus. She explained: *Well, I'm just not hungry for one because I grew up kind of malnourished and not knowing when my next meal would be. When kids grow up like that, they stop feeling hungry. So even if I can eat that day, I just forget because I don't get hungry and my friends will text me throughout the day, 'Hey did you eat?'* Isabelle, a 20-year-old Hispanic junior, said: *I still eat only 1 meal a day. That's how it was, and the food we did eat wasn't the healthiest. That experience probably made it easy now. It prepared me. It's not that much of a shock. 'Oh. I can't eat today.'*

Students also mentioned proactive strategies they took to reduce food insecurity. They noted that childhood experiences taught them to compare costs, choose cheaper food, and use coupons. One student was taught by her mother to watch for specials on Tuesdays and to let the store manager know if products were cheaper at different stores. Another student noted that she grew up eating very cheap food but made sure to eat vegetables. This experience shaped what she ate once she got to college. *I knew how to cope with it better than other students.*

Several students discussed their relationship with food. One student noted that she hid cans under her bed so her roommates could not find them. Others stressed their appreciation for the food they had and being conscious of not wasting any amount of food. Food insecure college students were often hesitant to buy too many fresh fruits and vegetables for fear of the produce going bad before they could eat it.

Finally, students who experienced food insecurity as children discussed budgeting, knowing how to keep food costs down, and hustling for food. Julia, a 23-year-old African-American senior, said: *I'm grateful for the struggle when I was younger because it's helped me know to pay bills first, and then whatever you have left, you do what you got to do. I also learned about food stamps. I used to look down on that when I was younger, but not now. The previous experience has shaped my current confidence. It made it so I know what to do as an adult.* Another student commented that she always found free food events on campus. She was not willing to spend money on food. *I'll get something if I'm starving, but that's always plan C. It's always been that way for me.*

Participants who experienced food insecurity as children have developed coping strategies that are slightly different than the overall research population. Analysis shows they focused more on what their parents taught them and also had a stronger sense of resolve about their situation. This does not mean, however, that they had less perceived mental health consequences of their food insecurity. Data shows that 62 percent of participants with childhood food insecurity had self-described mental health issues as a result of food insecurity while in college. Chapter 4 will discuss the association of physical and mental health with food insecurity in more detail.

References

Alaimo, Katherine, Christine M. Olson, and Edward A. Frongillo Jr. 2001. Food Insufficiency and American School-Aged Children's Cognitive, Academic, and Psychosocial Development. *Pediatrics* 108 (1): 44–53.

Allen, Alejandro C. 2019. *Study Hard, Eat Less: Exploring Food Insecurity Among College Students.* Master's Thesis, Texas State University. San Marcos, TX.

Broton, Katharine, and Sara Goldrick-Rab. 2018. Going Without: An Exploration of Food and Housing Insecurity Among Undergraduates. *Educational Researcher* 47 (2): 121–133. https://doi.org/10.3102/0013189x17741303.

Broton, Katharine, Kari Weaver, and Minhtuyen Mai. 2018. Hunger in Higher Education: Experiences and Correlates of Food Insecurity Among Wisconsin Undergraduates from Low-Income Families. *Social Sciences* 7 (10): 179. https://doi.org/10.3390/socsci7100179.

Bruening, Meg, Stephanie Brennhofer, Irene Van Woerden, Michael Todd, and Melissa Laska. 2016. Factors Related to the High Rates of Food Insecurity Among Diverse, Urban College Freshmen. *Journal of the Academy of Nutrition and Dietetics* 116 (9): 1450–1457. https://doi.org/10.1016/j.jand.2016.04.004.

Cady, Clare L. 2014. Food Insecurity as a Student Issue. *Journal of College and Character* 15 (4): 265–272. https://doi.org/10.1515/jcc-2014-0031.

Calvez, Kelsey, Caroline Miller, Lauren Thomas, Delma Vazquez, and Jayme Walenta. 2016. The University as a Site of Food Insecurity: Evaluating the Foodscape of Texas A&M University's Main Campus. *The Southwestern Geographer* 19: 1–14.

Cook, John, and Karen Jeng. 2009. *Child Food Insecurity: The Economic Impact of Our Nation.* Report. Feeding America. https://www.nokidhungry.org/sites/default/files/child-economy-study.pdf. Accessed 7 June 2018.

De Marco, M., S. Thorburn, and J. Due. 2009. In a Country as Affluent as America, People Should Be Eating: Experiences with and Perceptions of Food Insecurity Among Rural and Urban Oregonians. *Qualitative Health Research* 19 (7): 1010–1024. https://doi.org/10.1177/1049732309338868.

DeRuy, E. 2015. At Universities, More Students Are Working Full-Time. *The Atlantic,* October 28. https://www.theatlantic.com/politics/archive/2015/10/at-universities-more-students-are-working-full-time/433245/. Accessed 27 Apr 2019.

Dhillon, Jaapna, L. Karina Diaz Rios, Kaitlyn Aldaz, Natalie De La Cruz, Emily Vu, Syed Asad Asghar, Quintin Kuse, and Rudy Ortiz. 2019. We Don't Have a Lot of Healthy Options: Food Environment Perceptions of First-Year, Minority College Students Attending a Food Desert Campus. *Nutrients* 11 (4): 816. https://doi.org/10.3390/nu11040816.

Dubick, James, Brandon Mathews, and Clare Cady. 2016. *Hunger on Campus: The Challenge of Food Insecurity for College Students.* Report, October. http://studentsagainsthunger.org/wp-content/uploads/2016/10/Hunger_On_Campus.pdf. Accessed 10 May 2019.

El Zein, Aseel, Karla Shelnutt, Sarah Colby, Melissa Olfert, Kendra Kattelmann, Onikia Brown, Tandalayo Kidd, et al. 2017. The Prevalence of Food Insecurity and Its Association with Health and Academic Outcomes Among College Freshmen. *Advances in Nutrition* 8 (1): 4. https://doi.org/10.1093/advances/8.1.4.

El Zein, Aseel, Anne Mathews, Lisa House, and Karla Shelnutt. 2018. Why Are Hungry College Students Not Seeking Help? Predictors of and Barriers to Using an On-Campus Food Pantry. *Nutrients* 10 (9): 1163. https://doi.org/10.3390/nu10091163.

Farahbakhsh, Jasmine, Mahitab Hanbazaza, Geoff D.C. Ball, Anna P. Farmer, Katerina Maximova, and Noreen D. Willows. 2017. Food Insecure Student Clients of a University-Based Food Bank Have Compromised Health, Dietary Intake and Academic Quality. *Nutrition & Dietetics* 74 (1): 67–73. https://doi.org/10.1111/1747-0080.12307.

Forman, Michele R., Lauren D. Mangini, Yong Quan Dong, Ladia M. Hernandez, and Karen L. Fingerman. 2018. Food Insecurity and Hunger: Quiet Public Health Problems on Campus. *Journal of Nutrition & Food Sciences* 8 (2). https://doi.org/10.4172/2155-9600.1000668.

Freudenberg, Nicholas, Luis Manzo, Hollie Jones, Amy Kwan, Emma Tsui, and Monica Gagnon. 2011. *Food Insecurity at CUNY: Results from a Survey of CUNY Undergraduate Students.* Report. The Campaign for a Healthy CUNY, City University of New York, April. https://www.gc.cuny.edu/CUNY_GC/media/CUNY-Graduate-Center/PDF/Centers/CenterforHumanEnvironments/cunyfoodinsecurity.pdf. Accessed 29 April 2019.

Friedman, Zack. 2018. Student Loan Debt Statistics in 2018: A $1.5 Trillion Crisis. *Forbes*, October 26. https://www.forbes.com/sites/zackfriedman/2018/06/13/student-loan-debt-statistics-2018/#72594ae7310f. Accessed 18 May 2019.

Gaines, Alisha, Clifford A. Robb, Linda L. Knol, and Stephanie Sickler. 2014. Examining the Role of Financial Factors, Resources and Skills in Predicting Food Security Status Among College Students. *International Journal of Consumer Studies* 38 (4): 374–384. https://doi.org/10.1111/ijcs.12110.

Goldrick-Rab, Sara, Christine Baker-Smith, Vanessa Coca, Elizabeth Looker, and Tiffani Williams. 2019. *College and University Basic Needs Insecurity: A National #RealCollege Survey Report.* Report, April. https://hope4college.com/wp-content/uploads/2019/04/HOPE_realcollege_National_report_digital.pdf. Accessed 18 May 2019.

Government Accountability Office (GAO). 2018. *Better Information Could Help Eligible College Students Access Federal Food Assistance Benefits.* Report. U.S. Government Accountability Office, December. https://www.gao.gov/assets/700/696254.pdf. Accessed 18 May 2019.

Hager, Erin R., Alexandra Cockerham, Nicole O'Reilly, Donna Harrington, James Harding, Kristen M. Hurley, and Maureen M. Black. 2017. Food Swamps and Food Deserts in Baltimore City, MD, USA: Associations with Dietary Behaviours Among Urban Adolescent Girls. *Public Health Nutrition* 20 (14): 2598–2607. https://doi.org/10.1017/s1368980016002123.

Hanbazaza, M., G.D. Ball, A.P. Farmer, K. Maximova, J. Farahbakhsh, and N.D. Willows. 2017. A Comparison of Characteristics and Food Insecurity Coping Strategies Between International and Domestic Postsecondary Students Using a Food Bank Located on a University Campus. *Canadian Journal of Dietetic Practice and Research* 78 (4): 208–211.

Hanna, Lynn A. 2014. Hanna L: Evaluation of Food Insecurity Among College Students. *American International Journal of Contemporary Research* 4 (4): 46–49.

Hanson, Karla L., and Christine M. Olson. 2012. Chronic Health Conditions and Depressive Symptoms Strongly Predict Persistent Food Insecurity Among Rural Low-Income Families. *Journal of Health Care for the Poor and Underserved* 23 (3): 1174–1188.

Hattangadi, Nayantara, Ellen Vogel, Linda Carroll, and Pierre Côté. 2019. "Everybody I Know Is Always Hungry...But Nobody Asks Why": University Students, Food Insecurity and Mental Health. *Sustainability* 11 (6): 1571. https://doi.org/10.3390/su11061571.

Henry, Lisa. 2017. Understanding Food Insecurity Among College Students: Experience, Motivation, and Local Solutions. *Annals of Anthropological Practice* 41 (1): 6–19. https://doi.org/10.1111/napa.12108.

Kempson, Kathryn, Debra Palmer Keenan, Puneeta Sonya Sadani, and Audrey Adler. 2003. Maintaining Food Sufficiency: Coping Strategies Identified by Limited-Resource Individuals Versus Nutrition Educators. *Journal of Nutrition Education and Behavior* 35 (4): 179–188. https://doi.org/10.1016/s1499-4046(06)60332-1.

Lee, Sarah Dawn, Mahitab Hanbazaza, Geoff D.C. Ball, Anna Farmer, Katerina Maximova, and Noreen D. Willows. 2018. Food Insecurity Among Postsecondary Students in Developed Countries: A Narrative Review. *British Food Journal* 120 (11): 2660–2680. https://doi.org/10.1108/bfj-08-2017-0450.

Maroto, Maya E., Anastasia Snelling, and Henry Linck. 2015. Food Insecurity Among Community College Students: Prevalence and Association with Grade Point Average. *Community College Journal of Research and Practice* 39 (6): 515–526. https://doi.org/10.1080/10668926.2013.850758.

Martinez, Suzanna M., Karen Webb, Edward A. Frongillo, and Lorrene D. Ritchie. 2018. Food Insecurity in California's Public University System: What Are the Risk Factors? *Journal of Hunger & Environmental Nutrition* 13 (1): 1–18. https://doi.org/10.1080/19320248.2017.1374901.

McArthur, Laura Helena, Lanae Ball, Ariel C. Danek, and Donald Holbert. 2018. A High Prevalence of Food Insecurity Among University Students in Appalachia Reflects a Need for Educational Interventions and Policy Advocacy. *Journal of Nutrition Education and Behavior* 50 (6): 564–572. https://doi.org/10.1016/j.jneb.2017.10.011.

McIntyre, Lynn, N. Theresa Glanville, Kim D. Raine, Jutta B. Dayle, Bonnie Anderson, and Noreen Battaglia. 2003. Do Low-Income Lone Mothers Compromise Their Nutrition to Feed Their Children? *Canadian Medical Association Journal* 168 (6): 686–691.

McLaughlin, Katie, Jennifer Greif Green, Margarita Alegría, E. Jane Costello, Michael J. Gruber, Nancy A. Sampson, and Ronald Kessler. 2012. Food Insecurity and Mental Disorders in a National Sample of U.S. Adolescents. *Journal of the American Academy of Child & Adolescent Psychiatry* 51 (12): 1293–1303.

Meza, Anthony, Emily Altman, Suzanna Martinez, and Cindy W. Leung. 2018. "It's a Feeling That One Is Not Worth Food": A Qualitative Study Exploring the Psychosocial Experience and Academic Consequences of Food Insecurity Among College Students. *Journal of the Academy of Nutrition and Dietetics*, December 12. https://doi.org/10.1016/j.jand.2018.09.006.

Miles, Rhen, Bowen McBeath, Stephanie Brockett, and Paul Sorenson. 2017. Prevalence and Predictors of Social Work Student Food Insecurity. *Journal of Social Work Education* 53 (4): 651–663. https://doi.org/10.1080/1043779 7.2017.1299062.

Morris, Loran, Sylvia Smith, Jeremy Davis, and Dawn Bloyd Null. 2016. The Prevalence of Food Security and Insecurity Among Illinois University Students Response Letter. *Journal of Nutrition Education and Behavior* 48 (9): 376–382. https://doi.org/10.1016/j.jneb.2016.07.017.

Nazmi, Aydin, Suzanna Martinez, Ajani Byrd, Derrick Robinson, Stephanie Bianco, Jennifer Maguire, Rashida M. Crutchfield, Kelly Condron, and Lorrene Ritchie. 2018. A Systematic Review of Food Insecurity Among US Students in Higher Education. *Journal of Hunger & Environmental Nutrition*: 1–16. https://doi.org/10.1080/19320248.2018.1484316.

Patton-López, Megan M., Daniel F. López-Cevallos, Doris I. Cancel-Tirado, and Leticia Vazquez. 2014. Prevalence and Correlates of Food Insecurity Among

Students Attending a Midsize Rural University in Oregon. *Journal of Nutrition Education and Behavior* 46 (3): 209–214. https://doi.org/10.1016/j.jneb.2013.10.007.

Payne-Sturges, Devon C., Allison Tjaden, Kimberly M. Caldeira, Kathryn B. Vincent, and Amelia M. Arria. 2018. Student Hunger on Campus: Food Insecurity Among College Students and Implications for Academic Institutions. *American Journal of Health Promotion* 32 (2): 349–354. https://doi.org/10.1177/0890117117719620.

Pickett, William, Valerie Michaelson, and Colleen Davison. 2015. Beyond Nutrition: Hunger and Its Impact on the Health of Young Canadians. *International Journal of Public Health* 60 (5): 537–538. https://doi.org/10.1007/s00038-015-0673-z.

Radimer, Kathy Lynn. 1990. *Understanding Hunger and Developing Indicators to Assess It.* PhD Diss., Cornell University, Ithaca, NY.

Twill, Sarah E., Jacqueline Bergdahl, and Rebecca Fensler. 2016. Partnering to Build a Pantry: A University Campus Responds to Student Food Insecurity. *Journal of Poverty* 20 (3): 340–358. https://doi.org/10.1080/10875549.2015.1094775.

University of North Texas (UNT) Fact Sheet. 2017, Fall. https://institutionalresearch.unt.edu/sites/default/files/factsheet_2017-2018.pdf and https://institutionalresearch.unt.edu/fact-book/enrollment. Accessed 9 Oct 2018.

US Department of Agriculture Economic Research Service. 2017. Food Security in the U.S. Survey Tools. https://www.ers.usda.gov/topics/food-nutrition-assistance/food-security-in-the-us/survey-tools/#household.   Accessed 20 Sep 2018.

———. 2018. Food Security in the U.S. Measurement. https://www.ers.usda.gov/topics/food-nutrition-assistance/food-security-in-the-us/measurement/. Accessed 8 Sep 2018.

Watson, Tyler D., Hannah Malan, Deborah Glik, and Suzanna M. Martinez. 2017. College Students Identify University Support for Basic Needs and Life Skills as Key Ingredient in Addressing Food Insecurity on Campus. *California Agriculture* 71 (3): 130–138. https://doi.org/10.3733/ca.2017a0023.

Weaver, Robert R., Nicole A. Vaugh, Sean P. Hendricks, Penny E. McPherson-Myers, Qian Jia, Shari L. Willis, and Kevin P. Rescigo. 2019. University Student Food Insecurity and Academic Performance. *Journal of American College Health*, May 7. https://doi.org/10.1080/07448481.2019.1600522.

CHAPTER 3

Stigma and Shame

Abstract Stigma and Shame is a major focal point of my research. I begin with a discussion on Goffman's notion of shame and then move into a review of literature on the concept of shame as failure. Next, I provide an overview of the food insecurity and shame literature among college students. Since there are few studies that touch on stigma and shame in college, I expand this review to include the general population. Though no questions were asked directly about stigma or shame in the UNT research, it emerged as a predominant theme. I highlight the five sub-themes students discussed about stigma and shame. Next, I discuss college students' willingness to talk about their food insecurity with others. Finally, I highlight the potential to destigmatize food insecurity through increased awareness by university engagement with all students in a broad conversation about food insecurity and hunger on campus.

Keywords Food insecurity • Stigma • Shame • Conversation • Awareness

The stereotypical image of the starving college student surviving on instant Ramen noodles and peanut butter sandwiches is well known, but how close is the stereotype to reality? How does this stereotype affect perceptions of hunger issues in college among all students? Brandon, a 22-year-old White junior, noted: *But obviously, a lot of college students are*

© The Author(s) 2020

L. Henry, *Experiences of Hunger and Food Insecurity in College*,
https://doi.org/10.1007/978-3-030-31818-5_3

really short on cash or whatever. And I don't know. I just feel like sometimes it's played off as a joke. But it's actually pretty serious sometimes. You know? Allison, a 22-year-old White recent graduate, stated: *I think the general consensus with hunger on college campuses is 'Oh, you're just college students. You're eating Ramen.' That's what I thought it was until I got to college where I was like, I literally cannot afford food and then hunger is an actual thing. It's not just a broke college student thing. It's real.* Trinity, a 20-year-old African-American sophomore, added: *Everybody talks about how you're in college and you're going to starve. But it shouldn't happen like that because sometimes when you're hungry and you're in bed, you don't have energy to get up. You don't have energy to get up and make it to class. And I don't like people joking about it.*

In the pilot study of this research project (Henry 2017), students noted that food insecurity is faceless, has no standard image, and is often silent. "Students stated that having enough to eat and having no concerns about food is perceived as normal. Others stated that spending money on eating out and drinking beer is perceived as normal. Others stated that struggling to get by and eating cheap food is perceived as normal. For those who are food insecure, it is this paradox that contributes to confusion, shame, stigma, and fear" (2017, 11).

Social scientists have been studying shame since Goffman's seminal book in 1963, *Stigma: Notes on the Management of Spoiled Identity*. Goffman writes that shame can be externally judged by others or internalized and self-directed, both of which can lead to feelings of embarrassment and shame (Weaver and Trainer 2017). Weaver and Trainer (2017) build on Goffman's concept of self-directed stigma or self-stigma in a study on food insecurity, obesity, health, and stigma. Following Goffman, they contend that stigma is a unitary conception that "can be operationalized as *status incongruity*—this is, the potentially measurable difference between culturally held perceptions of what people should be or should achieve in a given realm, and what they are actually able to be or to achieve" (2017, 321). This remains true even when food insecurity is not visible to others. They go on to say "our own research on food insecurity points to the possibility that its most damaging impacts are not nutritional but rather psychological, deriving from external and internal shame and stigma associated with having to engage in non-normative food behaviors—in short, experiencing status incongruity" (2017, 322). Finally, Weaver and Trainer emphasize that stigma has negative physical and mental health consequences, which will be discussed in relation to food insecurity in Chap. 4.

Additional ethnographic research shows that food insecurity can be a marker of social failure, which leads to feelings of shame, stigma, and embarrassment, all of which can increase depression and anxiety (Weaver and Hadley 2009) (see Chap. 4 for depression and anxiety). Bernal et al. (2016) report that children experienced shame and embarrassment from not having adequate amounts of food and from needing food assistance. Connell et al. (2005) note that food insecure adolescents had a fear of judgment from others. Purdam et al. (2016) found similar results for food insecure adults.

Among the college population, research shows that food insecure students were faced with issues of stigma, embarrassment, feelings of awkwardness, shame, and guilt on a daily basis (Weaver and Hadley 2009; Nanama and Frongillo 2012; Cady 2014; Bahrampour 2014; Hoyt 2015; Kolowich 2015; Evans 2016; Henry 2017). Oftentimes students did not take advantage of food assistance programs because of the social stigma that is associated with acknowledging their food insecurity and asking for help (King 2017; Broton and Goldrick-Rab 2018; Hattangadi et al. 2019), as well as unawareness of such federally funded programs (Broton and Goldrick-Rab 2018). In a qualitative study at a Canadian university, Hattangadi et al. (2019) found that food insecure students associated their food insecurity with "a deep sense of failure, characterized by feelings of shame, frustration, and aloneness" (2019, 5). Furthermore, students discussed "feeling socially isolated, and personally responsible for their vulnerability" (2019, 5).

Allen and Alleman (2019) conducted an exploratory, qualitative study at an expensive, private university. They report that most students who struggle financially wanted to keep it secret from other students. Financially insecure students told lies to get out of social situations when they could not afford to socialize for fear of being discovered and experienced increased feelings of shame and embarrassment. Eating meals together is a way in which friends bond with each other, and food insecure students noted that it was embarrassing to say that you could not afford to go out, particularly at an affluent university where having money was the norm. A few food insecure students did find others who shared their financial and food situation. They found comfort and support in knowing that they were not completely alone.

In 2018, researchers from the University of South Florida wrote a technical report on teen food insecurity in Pinellas County (Burris et al. 2018). Teenagers, like college students, belong to a unique demographic category that is understudied. In this report, Burris et al. note that teenagers were acutely aware of their surroundings and often felt stigmatization and embarrassment about their food insecurity (Burris et al. 2018; see also Connell et al. 2005; Poppendieck 2010; Hamersma and Kim 2015; Popkin et al. 2016). This embarrassment often resulted in teenagers not asking for assistance and hiding their food insecurity (Popkin et al. 2016).

3.1   At the University of North Texas

In this research, topics related to stigma, shame, and embarrassment emerged as the most talked about theme, despite not asking a single question about stigma or shame. Five major sub-themes emerged from student stories—shame about being food insecure, social services and stigma, food secure students' perspectives, stigma and the food pantry, and childhood stigma.

3.1.1   Shame About Being Food Insecure

This sub-theme represents 32 percent of the discussion on shame and stigma. Food insecure students felt overwhelming feelings of shame, embarrassment, guilt, awkwardness, stigma, lack of pride, and unworthiness about being food insecure. They knew the stories of poor college students and understood that many people thought of college students as broke and hungry. However, this research sample was derived from a population of students who had already been to the UNT Food Pantry. They had already experienced a moment that was self-defined as low, a moment where they found themselves so desperate that they admitted to needing help. Congruent with Goffman (1963) and Weaver and Trainer (2017), it is the admission of not being able to provide for themselves that contributed to feelings of shame and embarrassment. Alexa, a 23-year-old African-American senior, noted:

> It's not a good feeling. It's kind of just like a feeling of just 'wow.' I can't even feed myself, you know? And it definitely messes with your ego. It definitely messes with your pride, but I had to put that aside. If you don't know the next time that you'll be able to eat a nice meal, or the next time you'll be able to cook

something, or if you'll be able to eat at all, you say 'what do I do now?' It took a long time for me to go to the food pantry. I had to put my pride aside. I know that it's probably all in my head, but feeling like you're less than, or that students don't have the same plight as you. Sometimes it's a bad feeling. I still feel bad if I call my parents for help. I feel like I need to do it on my own.

Jonathan is a 50-year-old American-Indian/White sophomore. He shared his thoughts by adding:

It was embarrassing to get free lunch as a child. It's embarrassing now as well, because a man is not supposed to get money from the government. A man's purpose is not to ask for help. I don't like talking about it. I carry a lot of shame over it because a man has three responsibilities—protect himself, protect his family, and protect his country. And right now, I can't do 2 of them, and that's very shameful to me.

Shame led students to hide their hunger from their classmates and friends. They did not want to ask them for help. They did not want pity. They did not want others feeling sorry for them. Julie is an 18-year-old White freshman. She said that she loved going out and being social with her friends, but *to go out and not order anything. That's very embarrassing. It's very hard to be social when you don't have money for it.* Molly, a 21-year-old White junior who lived on campus, also found it important to be social with her friends: *I decided that I need to budget for spending money for social events so I don't punish myself for, you know, not having enough money to buy stuff like that. I like being social. I like hanging out with my friends. So, I just budget a little for it.* Alexa shared her thoughts: *(laughs) yesterday in class my stomach started growling, so I'm like coughing over it, like (coughs). So, yeah, I definitely don't tell people about it. It's so embarrassing. I know other people get hungry, but I know that my hunger is because I can't eat.*

3.1.2   Social Services and Stigma

Social services are defined as services provided to the public by the government in order to benefit the community. For the purpose of this research, social services are considered to be those services that in some way provide relief to food insecure students, such as Supplemental Nutrition Assistant Program (SNAP), Special Supplemental Nutrition Program for *Women,*

Infants, and Children (WIC), or housing subsidies. As noted in Chap. 2, previous research found that about 20–41 percent of students with food insecurity received SNAP or other food-related public benefits (Broton and Goldrick-Rab 2018; Goldrick-Rab et al. 2019).

Because there was very little discussion of social services in the UNT pilot project (Henry 2017), current UNT participants were asked a range of questions about social services, including their experience, the experiences of other acquaintances or family members, general knowledge, opinions of services, ideas about who is served by the services, perceptions of people who use these services, and whether or not they would apply to receive benefits. Fifty-four percent of participants have had some experience with federal social services at some point in their lives.

Overall, opinions of social services were mostly positive among research participants. Students spoke about social services as good, helpful programs. Some explained that these services are in place to help people through a rough time or to get back on their feet. A few of the students mentioned peoples' right to be able to eat. Cassandra, a 20-year-old African-American sophomore, explained:

> *I think food is a definite that people should have. I think it shouldn't be a privilege. I think it should be a right. I think people should always have access to fresh food … but it's not that easy, that's all I can say. Because there are other things that come up, people lose their jobs, like me. People, you know, they have other things that are going on. They are trying to better their lives. They are in school. There are so many other variables that come to play that have nothing to do with money that affects people's lives and puts them in that position.*

Despite conversations about social services being helpful, much of the discussion surrounding social services also included topics of stigma and shame, representing 26 percent of the discussion on this theme (see Chap. 6 for more discussion of social services). Many students grew up being embarrassed about their families using social services, and these feelings carried over into their college experience. Interestingly, students who talked about the benefits of the system supporting people in need almost simultaneously pointed out the stigma surrounding the use of social services and how some people abuse the system. They drew a distinction between those who really needed the services and those who were taking advantage of the system. Corbin, a 19-year-old African-American freshman who lived on campus, gave this analogy: *Using social services is like a batch of grapes. You have the whole batch of grapes, but you're gonna have loose grapes. You know, those loose grapes are the people that take advantage of it. You know, the batch, the batch that stays together is the people who need it. They need it, you know what I'm saying?* Abuses that were specifically mentioned included pretending to be unable to make enough money and selling benefits to others for cash. Participants explained that some people are lazy and do not want to work, so they abuse the system. Some participants also noted that people who abuse the system should be penalized, that there need to be stricter regulations, or that the services should be provided in the form of a loan that must be paid back.

Participants also spoke about stigma directed toward the people who use social services, including themselves. Susan is 22 years old, White, and recently graduated. She explained: *I think that takes a lot of your pride away to go and apply for those services sometimes. One time, I thought about applying. I started the application process for food stamps, but I didn't follow through. Mostly I guess just the stigma of it, you know? I wanted to be secure enough to pay for it by myself.* They pointed out the difficulty in qualifying for services followed by how embarrassed they were to use their LoneStar (Texas benefit card) or WIC card. Chloe, a 20-year-old multiethnic junior, noted: *I've been food insecure my entire life so I think using food stamps is normal, but if I'm with a friend who doesn't know about them or has never seen them, then I try to hide the SNAP card. People who don't use them view people who do use them with weird looks ... that you are a strange person.* A few students noted that there is even a stigma around how the money is spent. The people using the services seem to be aware that their spending may seem negligent to outsiders, but they shared that there are good reasons to spend the money as they do. Sophia is a 22-year-old Hispanic junior who lived on campus. She explained: *There are times when people are like, you know, 'I'm going to have to make this money last. So, I'm going to buy the cheapest thing possible for my kids because of quantity and not quality.' And that can cause health issues like diabetes and stuff. You know, it's just another issue, but it's very complex.*

Research participants also compared people who use social services to themselves. When they talked about their perceptions of people who used social services, they often talked about stigma as an added concern in their lives. Melissa is a 34-year-old White junior who shared: *It wasn't really my fault. I mean, maybe I made some mistakes, could have done something better, but when it came down to it, there was no money for so long. There wouldn't have been another choice. But I can't hold it against people, I guess. And if I would overhear somebody saying something derogatory, they're probably not going to be my friend if they would talk badly about things like that. You know, I just wouldn't.* Participants noted that people who need to use social services were in a difficult situation and were smart to use resources to help their situation. Lucy, a 21-year-old White sophomore, said: *Probably they are just having some financial problems. I mean, I know a lot of people have really bad misconceptions about it, but I feel that a lot of people haven't been in that situation, when people look down on other people for buying junk food, cheap food. What do they expect people to eat? You're not gonna buy stale bread and water.*

Students who gave responses with the greatest reference to stigma were the group of students who have never experienced using social services and were not food insecure as children.

3.1.3   Food Secure Students' Perceptions

This sub-theme represents 15 percent of the discussion on shame and stigma. This section reflects food insecure students' thoughts on the perceptions of <u>food secure students</u> about food insecurity and hunger on campus. Food insecure participants reported a lack of understanding and empathy from food secure students on what it is like to struggle to get enough food to eat. They think food secure students perceive them as poor, low-income, dirty, unhealthy, lazy, unfortunate, unfocused, depressed, less motivated, unaware of money management, and just not trying hard enough. There was a general sense that wealthier, food secure students looked down on lower-income classmates and thought they were better because of their wealth. There was also a perception that wealthier students did not understand that some parents absolutely could not help children with college finances. Meza et al. (2018) report similar patterns in their qualitative study at the University of California at Berkeley. Their participants noted a lack of understanding from food secure students and projected feelings of jealousy and resentment. Melissa shared her thoughts:

Yes, I think it carries a stigma for them (food secure students). They think we're hungry because we've done something wrong. Maybe I've made some mistakes, but there was never enough money. The first few times I went to the food pantry, I took only about 2–4 meals because I didn't want to take too much. I am sure there are people out there that are worse off; someone needs it more. I think the experience in the pantry is very welcoming. If someone thinks there is stigma with going there ... I don't think there is because the worker doesn't go in with you and watch. I've been to lots of food pantries so I'm not scared or embarrassed anymore.

Chloe added: *Food secure students think we are dirty. There is shame. Others don't absorb sympathetic feelings so they try to avoid people who are suffering through stuff like this because they don't want to feel bad for what they have.*

3.1.4   Stigma and the Food Pantry

This sub-theme represents 15 percent of the discussion on shame and stigma. Many students stated fear of judgment and stigma from their peers, as well as the university, as an obstacle they faced before their first visit to the pantry. First-time users of the pantry were extremely nervous. However, many of these same patrons expressed relief from those fears even after their first visit. They explained that the staff's interactions put them at ease. They appreciated the confidentiality offered to them by the pantry sign-in process and lack of judgment they felt from the staff. Susan noted: *The first time I went, I didn't get as much food as the second time I went. I was a very nervous about it. I didn't want people to see me carrying out the bag of food. The second time I went, I was more confident AND there was more food so I took more.* However, despite feeling more confident and less embarrassed, many students disliked being escorted from the Dean of Students department on the fourth floor to the food pantry on the third floor by a member of the Dean of Students staff. A few students referred to it as the "walk of shame." Jacob, a 30-year-old South Asian international graduate student, explained: *I didn't like having to go to the Dean of Students, then walking downstairs to the food pantry. There are a lot of students around. At first, I thought the food pantry was going to be more open and that you could just walk in. Consider putting the food pantry in a different location where students don't have to check in with the Dean of Students upstairs first.* Other students noted that walking through the University Union with a bag full of groceries was embarrassing. *Nobody else leaves the union like that. Only students who have been to the pantry* (see Chap. 6 for a more detailed evaluation of the UNT Food Pantry).

3.1.5   Childhood Stigma

This sub-theme represents seven percent of the overall discussion on shame and stigma. Of the participants who experienced food insecurity of children (58%), 25 percent of them reflected on feelings of stigma, shame, and embarrassment—particularly regarding grocery shopping, food pantries, and school lunches. Students noted embarrassment about going to the grocery store with their food stamps and WIC coupons. Joe, a 34-year-old White senior, noted: *It was embarrassing when I was a kid because everyone would know. I remember once we were at Kroger and a kid from my class was in the next line. That was really embarrassing because there was a hold up in the line. There is stigma with food stamps in general. You think poverty. You think of people working the system. It's been equated to a lady with 5 kids and a crack head at that.* Jade, a 20-year-old Asian junior, stated that it was more embarrassing for her mother. She used to pretend that it was no big deal so her mom would feel better. Other students discussed stigma about going to the food pantry. *It was embarrassing to go to the food pantry in my little town when I was in high school. We went a few times and I knew people there so I was so embarrassed.* Participants also talked about stigma in school. One student noted that she used to eat other kids' leftovers in the cafeteria, and while she cared about the stigma, she was too hungry to stop. Many participants noted that schools used to have the free and reduce-priced lunch kids line up separately, and this caused a tremendous amount of stress and embarrassment. Destiny is a 21-year-old African-American junior whose family is from Nigeria. She shared: *My friends were in the line getting good vegetables, and I was in the free lunch line getting gross vegetables. My peers were getting things that I wanted. In high school the lines were divided. Fortunately, there were other people in the line with me, but it really splits you up according to class. I was aware of it, but I didn't let it define me socially. It was still hard.*

The majority of participants who reflected on childhood stigma also noted that they did not feel the same level of stigma as adults. Cameron, who did not share demographic information, stated that when they were younger, peers would ask questions such as *is your mom on drugs? why don't you get a job? what's wrong with you? you're broke and a bum.* These words were demoralizing growing up, but she represents the pattern of food insecure college students who are better able to manage their feelings of shame as adults because of the experiences they had as children.

3.2   Conversations About Food Insecurity

Pilot research indicated that the majority of food insecure college students did not share their struggles with others (Henry 2017). In this study, I intentionally asked participants about their willingness to discuss and talk about their food insecurity with others.

Fifty-nine percent said they did not talk to others about food insecurity issues and cited shame, embarrassment, and pride as the primary reasons. Smaller patterns emerged that included not wanting to worry their family or be a burden to others, not wanting to share their personal problems, not wanting pity, and feelings of jealousy. Meza et al. (2018) also found that students at Berkley did not want to disappoint their families. Erika, a 19-year-old White sophomore, shared: *I don't talk about it because it's embarrassing. My mom was mad that I didn't talk to her. I thought it was my fault that I couldn't afford food, but I didn't have time for another job. My mom didn't want me to take food away from people 'who really needed it,' but I really needed it.* Tyron, a 19-year-old African-American freshman who lived on campus, said: *I never talk about it. Somebody always has it worse.* James, a 20-year-old African-American sophomore, explained: *We are college students and we're supposed to be hungrier sometimes. So that's like how I thought of it, so I didn't really treat it as like a serious problem my freshman year.*

This notion of pride extends to embarrassment around their friends. Most food insecure students did not want their friends to know about their hunger and financial issues. This resulted in hesitation to socialize, a strain on social relationships, and feelings of isolation. One Hispanic student noted that her reluctance to talk to others stemmed from her fear that others would stereotype her because of her ethnicity. Often the topic of food insecurity in conversation was highly avoided, which reinforced the silence of food insecurity among students. Food insecure students miss out on many social interactions, which are often seen as a critical piece of the college experience at certain universities (see also Meza et al. 2018).

Forty-one percent said they had a trusted family member, a roommate, or a small group of friends (many in a similar situation) with whom they could share their struggles about food insecurity issues. Students who were the most open about their food insecurity and would talk to anyone about their struggles tended to be majoring in disciplines that emphasize communication, such as social work. Camila, a 22-year-old Hispanic senior, noted: *I tell some of my friends. Sometimes they take me grocery shopping, and it makes me feel not as alone. It's a shared frustration, and honestly, is kind of maybe bonding.* I hypothesized that students who experienced food insecurity as children would be more likely to have conversations about food insecurity in college. However, there is no pattern. The strongest pattern found to date for students communicating about food insecurity relates to their major. One student said, *closed mouths don't get fed.* Research shows that social support is a key strategy in coping with food insecurity that may decrease some of the negative impacts on physical and mental health (see Chap. 4; Dirks and Carter 1980; Martin et al. 2004; Higashi et al. 2017; Watson et al. 2017). Watson et al. (2017) show that college students who prepare communal meals together experienced feelings of inclusion and social support, which reduces stress and anxiety. Communal dining can be an effective coping strategy for food insecurity. Allen and Alleman (2019) show that not all social interactions were negative. Food insecure students at Status U found comfort in social relationships with other students who had food struggles, particularly because Status U is an affluent university and these students did not fit the norm.

3.3   DESTIGMATIZATION THROUGH AWARENESS

During the interview, we asked participants if they would like to see the university engage in a broader conversation about food insecurity on campus. An overwhelming majority (94%) agreed that a broader conversation coming from the university would be beneficial. From there, the conversation branched into two themes—reducing stigma and increasing knowledge of resources. Participants stressed that having a university conversation about hunger would reduce stigma by bringing people together, opening up the conversation, and educating the entire campus community about the various issues around hunger and food insecurity in college. In addition to food insecurity, participants would like the campus to discuss other topics, such as healthy eating, mental health, poverty, and multiculturalism. Students know these can be sensitive topics, and they believe that more campus dialog will decrease negative perspectives and increase understanding for all students. Michael is a 21-year-old Asian/White junior. He explained: *A greater conversation on campus could really reduce the stigma and awkwardness about going to the pantry. The more we can talk about it, about it as a possible solution, the less embarrassing it will be for people.*

TJ, a 21-year-old White junior, said:

I think being hungry affects more than just one person. A lot of other students struggle with it. And the fact that I think it's embarrassing to talk about it means that I could have friends that do the same thing, but none of us are talking about it because it's not something that's ever brought up.

Sophia shared: *Just making people more consciously aware that sometimes people don't have the money to buy food. Sometimes people are financially struggling, obviously, and other students need to know this exists on campus.*

Participants also stressed that more information about available resources that are beneficial to all students is needed. University administrators and staff often think they are putting out a tremendous amount of information about resources. While this might be true, students were not receiving those messages, and they admitted that they were often not paying attention. Students are bombarded with information in college, not only in the classroom but also from e-mails and flyers. Students admitted to needing multiple, repeated messaging in order for information to soak in. Most students wanted more information in the form of signs, billboards, and bumper stickers. Others suggested posting more information at the library mall, including tabling events where students could pick up information and swag as they passed by. Other information outlets mentioned include social media messages (including hashtags), presentations to classes, flyers in dorms, programs by resident assistants, programs during orientation, and information on syllabi. Makayla, a 20-year-old African-American junior, said:

Well, I don't know how they do orientation now. I've been in college for a little while, but when I went to orientation, we were in smaller groups, and we only talked about academics ... like the academic services on campus. We never talked about the counselor and testing center or the clinic. We never talked about like the common club or the food pantry. We never talked about anything like that. I feel like that should be talked about more, because those are services that people are more so going to go to than the learning center. No offense, this is college, but those things are real life.

The university does host canned food drives for library fines and parking tickets. Participants suggested even more events such as additional food drives, toiletry drives, Greek Life food drives, seminars, conferences, and peer mentoring. One student suggested: "Instead of 'Food for Fines' make the campaign 'Food for Friends!' or 'Soup for Students!'"

REFERENCES

Allen, Cara Cliburn, and Nathan F. Alleman. 2019. A Private Struggle at a Private Institution: Effects of Student Hunger on Social and Academic Experiences. *Journal of College Student Development* 60 (1): 52–69. https://doi.org/10.1353/csd.2019.0003.

Bahrampour, Tara. 2014. More College Students Battle Hunger as Education and Living Costs Rise. *The Washington Post*, April 9. https://www.washingtonpost.com/local/more-college-students-battle-hunger-as-education-and-living-costs-rise/2014/04/09/60208db6-bb63-11e3-9a05-c739f29ccb08_story.html. Accessed 4 Oct 2016.

Bernal, Jennifer, Edward A. Frongillo, and Klaus Jaffe. 2016. Food Insecurity of Children and Shame of Others Knowing They Are Without Food. *Journal of Hunger & Environmental Nutrition* 11 (2): 180–194. https://doi.org/10.1080/19320248.2016.1157543.

Broton, Katharine, and Sara Goldrick-Rab. 2018. Going Without: An Exploration of Food and Housing Insecurity Among Undergraduates. *Educational Researcher* 47 (2): 121–133. https://doi.org/10.3102/0013189x17741303.

Burris, Mecca, Sarah Bradley, David Himmelgreen, Kayla Rykiel, Paige Tucker, Danielle Hintz, and Elisa Shannon. 2018. Teen Food Insecurity in Pinellas County Technical Report, May 19. https://www.jwbpinellas.org/wp-content/uploads/2018/06/Teen-food-insecurity-in-Pinellas-County_Technical-Report_5-21-2018.pdf. Accessed 17 May 2019.

Cady, Clare L. 2014. Food Insecurity as a Student Issue. *Journal of College and Character* 15 (4): 265–272. https://doi.org/10.1515/jcc-2014-0031.

Connell, Carol L., Kristi L. Lofton, Kathy Yadrick, and Timothy A. Rehner. 2005. Children's Experiences of Food Insecurity Can Assist in Understanding Its Effect on Their Well-Being. *The Journal of Nutrition* 135 (7): 1683–1690. https://doi.org/10.1093/jn/135.7.1683.

Dirks, Robert, and James P. Carter. 1980. Social Responses during Severe Food Shortages and Famine. *Current Anthropology* 21 (1): 21–44. https://doi.org/10.1016/b978-0-08-027998-5.50017-9.

Evans, Brooke A. 2016. Homeless and Hungry in College. *Change: The Magazine of Higher Education* 48 (1): 26–29.

Goffman, Erving. 1963. *Stigma: Notes on the Management of Spoiled Identity*. New York, NY: Simon & Schuster.

Goldrick-Rab, Sara, Christine Baker-Smith, Vanessa Coca, Elizabeth Looker, and Tiffani Williams. 2019. *College and University Basic Needs Insecurity: A National #RealCollege Survey Report*. Report, April. https://hope4college.com/wp-content/uploads/2019/04/HOPE_realcollege_National_report_digital.pdf. Accessed 18 May 2019.

Hamersma, S., and M. Kim. 2015. Food Security and Teenage Labor Supply. *Applied Economic Perspectives and Policy*: 73–92, March 31. https://doi.org/10.1093/aepp/ppv007.

Hattangadi, Nayantara, Ellen Vogel, Linda Carroll, and Pierre Côté. 2019. "Everybody I Know Is Always Hungry...But Nobody Asks Why": University Students, Food Insecurity and Mental Health. *Sustainability* 11 (6): 1571. https://doi.org/10.3390/su11061571.

Henry, Lisa. 2017. Understanding Food Insecurity Among College Students: Experience, Motivation, and Local Solutions. *Annals of Anthropological Practice* 41 (1): 6–19. https://doi.org/10.1111/napa.12108.

Higashi, Robin T., Simon Craddock Lee, Carla Pezzia, Lisa Quirk, Tammy Leonard, and Sandi L. Pruitt. 2017. Family and Social Context Contributes to the Interplay of Economic Insecurity, Food Insecurity, and Health. *Annals of Anthropological Practice* 41 (2): 67–77. https://doi.org/10.1111/napa.12114.

Hoyt, Elizabeth. 2015. Food Insecurity is the New Hunger & It's Prevalent on U.S. College Campuses. *Fastweb*. http://www.fastweb.com/student-life/articles/food-insecurity-prevalent-on-college-campuses. Accessed 15 Sep 2016.

King, Jennifer A. 2017. *Food Insecurity Among College Students—Exploring the Predictors of Food Assistance Resource Use*. PhD Diss., Kent State University.

Kolowich, Steve. 2015. How Many College Students Are Going Hungry? *The Chronicle of Higher Education*, November 3. http://www.chronicle.com/article/how-many-college-students-are/234033. Accessed 3 Oct 2016.

Martin, Katie S., Beatrice L. Rogers, John T. Cook, and Hugh M. Joseph. 2004. Social Capital Is Associated with Decreased Risk of Hunger. *Social Science & Medicine* 58 (12): 2645–2654. https://doi.org/10.1016/j.socscimed.2003.09.026.

Meza, Anthony, Emily Altman, Suzanna Martinez, and Cindy W. Leung. 2018. "It's a Feeling That One is Not Worth Food": A Qualitative Study Exploring the Psychosocial Experience and Academic Consequences of Food Insecurity Among College Students. *Journal of the Academy of Nutrition and Dietetics*, December 12. https://doi.org/10.1016/j.jand.2018.09.006.

Nanama, Siméon, and Edward A. Frongillo. 2012. Altered Social Cohesion and Adverse Psychological Experiences with Chronic Food Insecurity in the Non-market Economy and Complex Households of Burkina Faso. *Social Science & Medicine* 74 (3): 444–451. https://doi.org/10.1016/j.socscimed.2011.11.009.

Popkin, Susan J., Molly M. Scott, and Martha Galvez. 2016. *Impossible Choices: Teens and Food Insecurity in America*. Report. Washington, DC: Urban Institute and Feeding America. https://www.urban.org/sites/default/files/alfresco/publication-pdfs/2000914-Impossible-Choices-Teens-and-Food-Insecurity-in-America.pdf.

Poppendieck, Janet. 2010. *Free for All: Fixing School Food in America*. Berkeley, CA: University of California Press.

Purdam, Kingsley, Elisabeth A. Garratt, and Aneez Esmail. 2016. Hungry? Food Insecurity, Social Stigma and Embarrassment in the UK. *Sociology* 50 (6): 1072–1088. https://doi.org/10.1177/0038038515594092.

Watson, Tyler D., Hannah Malan, Deborah Glik, and Suzanna M. Martinez. 2017. College Students Identify University Support for Basic Needs and Life Skills as Key Ingredient in Addressing Food Insecurity on Campus. *California Agriculture* 71 (3): 130–138. https://doi.org/10.3733/ca.2017a0023.

Weaver, Lesley Jo, and Craig Hadley. 2009. Moving Beyond Hunger and Nutrition: A Systematic Review of the Evidence Linking Food Insecurity and Mental Health in Developing Countries. *Ecology of Food and Nutrition* 48 (4): 263–284. https://doi.org/10.1080/03670240903001167.

Weaver, Lesley Jo, and Sarah Trainer. 2017. Shame, Blame, and Status Incongruity: Health and Stigma in Rural Brazil and the Urban United Arab Emirates. *Culture, Medicine, and Psychiatry* 41 (3): 319–340. https://doi.org/10.1007/s11013-016-9518-3.

CHAPTER 4

Physical Health, Mental Health, and Nutrition

Abstract This chapter begins with a literature review on the negative health outcomes associated with food insecurity and poor dietary habits in the general population. I briefly review the literature on K-12 students before detailing the expanding research on college students. Next, I discuss the research at UNT and detail the physical consequences of food insecurity as described by students. The next section discusses the association of mental health issues with hunger and poor nutrition, starting with the general literature, then among college student, and next among UNT students. Finally, I end the chapter with a discussion about how nutrition fits in with their experiences with food insecurity and their physical and mental health.

Keywords Food insecurity • Nutrition • Physical health • Mental health

Sometimes I feel like I'll faint if I walk too much on campus, or I feel like I'm going to faint if I'm taking a shower. If I'm doing anything that's like too active and I'm not able to eat a meal that day, then I feel really exhausted and tired. (Gabriela, 21-year-old, Hispanic, junior)

A specific research goal of this study was to investigate the association of physical and mental health with food insecurity among college students. Participants were asked a series of qualitative interview questions about nutrition, access to nutritious food, medical or dietary expenses that impacted their ability to buy enough food, and *if* and how food insecurity has impacted their physical and/or mental health. The open-ended nature of the questions allowed participants to discuss any aspect of these issues. They were not guided, nor prompted beyond the initial questions. Importantly, student responses represent their perceptions and lived experiences of being hungry and food insecure and how it impacted their bodies—physically, mentally, and emotionally. No official health data was collected.

4.1   Physical Health, Hunger, and Poor Nutrition

There is extensive literature that highlights the negative health outcomes associated with food insecurity. A 2018 review of the U.S. literature shows food insecurity linked to cardiovascular disease, hypertension, diabetes, and infectious diseases (Arenas et al. 2018). In a second 2018 systematic review of the literature, Weaver and Fasel (2018) examined 51 studies and found a positive relationship between food insecurity and chronic disease. Fifteen of these studies controlled for body mass index (BMI) in order to eliminate some level of obesity as a factor for chronic disease. Of the 15 studies that limited obesity as a contributing factor, 14 found a direct positive relationship between food insecurity and chronic disease, namely type 2 diabetes, asthma, and dyslipidemia. Furthermore, low socio-economic status was the strongest predictor of the relationship (see also Seligman et al. 2010). Higashi et al. (2015) also report multiple co-morbidities (high blood pressure, diabetes, arthritis, depression, and anxiety) among low-income food insecure households.

Food insecurity is strongly associated with poor dietary habits that consist of low vegetable, fruit, and fiber intake and high consumption of energy-dense foods—a low nutrition diet. Hadley and Crooks (2012) argue that context-specific coping strategies for food insecurity may have short-term and long-term impacts on nutritional well-being and physical and mental health. Their extensive review of the literature highlights multiple examples and patterns. In high-income countries with food safety nets, such as the U.S., the shift to less expensive foods leads to consumption of increased energy-dense and nutrient-poor foods (Dietz 1995; Basiotis and Lino 2002; Adams et al. 2003; Darmon et al. 2004; Leung et al. 2014). This trend is associated with overnutrition and weight gain rather than a significant reduction in total calories, particularly among women (Olson 1999; Townsend et al. 2001; Basiotis and Lino 2002; Adams et al. 2003). The link between food insecurity and obesity is so well-documented that the American Diabetic Association now considers food insecurity as a risk factor for developing diabetes because of its association with obesity (Dinour et al. 2007; Finney et al. 2010; Ivers and Cullen 2011; Franklin et al. 2012; Hadley and Crooks 2012; Ashe and Sonnino 2013; Laraia 2013; Weaver and Fasel 2018). Furthermore, lack of resources may also force individuals or households to forgo medications, other medical treatments, or eat a diet not in compliance with their medical condition when faced with competing financial demands (Quandt and Rao 1999; Hadley and Crooks 2012).

The negative nutritional and health impacts of food insecurity on children and adolescents are also well-documented. According to Knowles et al. (2015), the "health consequences of food insecurity include poor cognitive, social, and emotional development among young children (Rose-Jacobs et al. 2008; Frank et al. 2010), suicidal ideation among adolescents (Alaimo et al. 2002); [and] depressive symptoms (Casey et al. 2004; Whitaker et al. 2006)" (Knowles et al. 2015, 255–256). As summarized by Burris et al. (2018), these negative outcomes include "frequent stomach aches, cold, headaches, and hospitalizations, lower bone mineral content in adolescent boys, stunting, wasting, nutrient deficiencies such as iron deficiency anemia among adolescents, impaired social and behavioral issues, lower mental proficiency, depression and anxiety, and lower school achievements (Coleman-Jensen et al. 2012; Himmelgreen 2013; Hamrick and McClelland 2016; Whitaker et al. 2006)" (2018, 11; see also Himmelgreen et al. 2000; Chilton et al. 2007; Rose-Jacobs et al. 2008; Kirkpatrick and Tarasuk 2008; Weinstein et al. 2009). Research also shows that food insecure adolescents consume foods high in sugar and fat and low in vegetables, which can have longer-term negative consequences of obesity and poor food habits into adulthood (Fram et al. 2015; Hamrick and McClelland 2016). Hadley and Crooks (2012) contend that food insecure families may engage in trade-offs between competing food and non-food demands, which ultimately may impact nutrition and health outcomes.

4.1.1   Among College Students

The small but growing literature on food insecurity among college students shows similar patterns of poor nutrition and related health consequences (Hughes et al. 2011; Patton-López et al. 2014; Bruening et al. 2016; Farahbakhsh et al. 2017; Mirabitur et al. 2016; Henry 2017; Knol et al. 2017; Broton et al. 2018; Bruening et al. 2018; Payne-Sturges et al. 2018; Dhillon et al. 2019; Allen and Alleman 2019). Although mental health will be discussed in more detail later, it is difficult to separate out the co-contributing factors of poor nutrition, lack of time, eating cheap, fast, convenient foods that are full of high fats and sugars, and stress among college students. According to the American Academy of Pediatrics, "toxic stress of food insecurity in early life leads to chronic diseases such as cardiovascular diseases, cancers, asthma, and autoimmune disease" (Greene 2018, 3; see also Garner et al. 2012). Meza et al. (2018) report that food insecure students in California can afford only foods low in nutrition which contributes to increased stress, which leads to diminished physical health outcomes. Dhillon et al. (2019) report that lack of affordability and poor accessibility of nutritious food for college students contributes to their choice of low-nutrient food sources.

4.1.2   At the University of North Texas

Food insecure students at the University of North Texas recognized the physical effects of limited calorie consumption and eating nutritiously poor food. The overwhelming majority (83%) discussed some type of impact on their physical health. Four themes emerged from these open-ended discussions:

- lack of energy
- poor nutrition
- specific health symptoms
- weight issues

Lack of energy was the most commonly discussed physical issue. Eighty-three percent of participants mentioned having low energy and being physically tired. Roughly half of these students (51%) discussed having low energy because they did not eat enough. Several students (8%) specifically discussed not being able to work out or play sports because they "didn't have enough calories" to spend on physical activity. The other half of students attributed their low energy to poor nutrition (see further discussion below). Gabriela shared another experience about her low energy: *If I don't have enough energy to get up and go to class, and I know that I'm not going to be able to get food on campus, sometimes I feel too scared to go to class, so I don't push it and I just stay home.* Cameron explained:

> *My energy levels for sure. Because like I would have classes back to back, and I didn't have any portable food because I would just have canned food. So, I would be really hungry, but I couldn't use the food that I got at the pantry because I had nowhere to heat it up or keep it, or whatever. So sometimes I would be really hungry in class and just have no energy at all.*

Natalie, a 20-year-old Hispanic senior, shared: *I remember during periods of food insecurity. I would be very groggy and lethargic, you know? I would go to my classes and then I would come home and just sleep.* Beverly, a 21-year-old African-American junior, talked about not wanting to get out of bed:

> *When I started eating really bad, I gained 20 pounds at least. I was a lot smaller last summer. I felt very sluggish and lazy and tired all the time, so I would just stay in bed. My sleep schedule was just off. I was missing classes. I would just literally want to lay in bed all day and sleep or just lay there and watch TV. And, I just wouldn't go to class. I was waking up at 2:00 p.m. and going to bed at 3:00 a.m., so that also affected my health.*

Regina, a 19-year-old African-American sophomore, shared her thoughts on nutrition and energy: *Your body needs nutrition to do excessive exercise and stuff. I used to be in volleyball and all these other activities. My body's mad at me. I stopped that phase of my life because taking care of my food became a top priority. I need to study and stuff like that so I can graduate on time.*

In Chap. 2, I discussed sleeping as a coping strategy for dealing with hunger. During discussions of physical health, participants discussed sleeping in relation to their physical exhaustion. Students reported "sleeping for days," sleeping more than usual, and being hard to wake up (see also Meza et al. 2018). Trinity, a 20-year-old African-American sophomore, explained: *So, whenever that happens, I really try to sleep for a meal, like sleep for dinner, sleep for breakfast.* Sophia, a 22-year-old Hispanic junior who lived on campus, talked about her experience with sleep:

I remember sometimes that it would be very hard to sleep. I remember just being hungry, and just being in the room that I was staying in. And I couldn't sleep...to the point where I would stay up the whole night. That caused a lot of migraines and stuff. That's all I can remember, just not focusing, obviously, because I wasn't resting. But whenever I would sleep, I would knock out. My boyfriend would be like, 'Wake up. Wake up. Wake up.' and I couldn't wake up. I was very tired, trying to sleep, not being able to. Um, so just being very stressed, very, very uptight. Like I remember just being like (groans) very tight from my shoulders all the time.

Poor nutrition emerged as the second-largest theme (33%) when participants discussed the physical effects of hunger and food insecurity. Participants talked about the great expense of groceries. They bought as little as possible and often skipped meals. They could afford only nutrient-poor, highly processed food. They purchased food that was from cheap brands, was long-lasting, could be stretched, and was on sale. They acknowledged that the food they ate was low in nutritional value, but they could not afford fresh food that would spoil quickly. Molly, a 23-year-old White junior who lived on campus, noted: *Oh boy. It's really hard to stay healthy whenever you're poor, I guess. Like I try to make healthier decisions. I try to eat more vegetables and stuff. But I'll eat what I have.*

Importantly, participants directly associated poor nutrition and hunger with their physical symptoms of lack of energy (as noted above), getting sick, and weight issues. Thirty-three percent of participants mentioned specific nutrient deficiencies (such as potassium, iron, vitamin D, and vitamin A) and specific illnesses or health conditions, such as kidney stones, weak immune system, high blood pressure, high cholesterol, eye soreness, dehydration, poor skin, headaches, stomach aches, digestive issues, poor circulation, cavities, joint pain, bronchitis, loss of muscle, muscle cramps, feeling hazy or dizzy, and fainting. Ana, a 22-year-old African-American junior, noted: *All I ate were noodles and I got very, very, very sick. I didn't have any energy. I wasn't getting any nutrients that I needed. I had low energy and my head was foggy.* Vanessa, a 21-year-old African-American junior, insisted: *I got the flu from skipping meals. I know I did. Poor nutrition weakened my immune system and I got the flu. I told myself to take a break, to re-evaluate my life. I told myself that I need to eat more and to sleep more.* Weight issues were mentioned by 27 percent of participants as a consequence of food insecurity. Of those who mentioned weight issues, 48 percent mentioned weight loss, 28 percent mentioned weight gain from eating a poor diet, and 24 percent mentioned frequent fluctuations in weight.

As discussed in Chap. 2, students who experienced food insecurity as children seem to have a strong sense of resolve or coping. One student said he felt no physical effect from being food insecure because he has always been hungry. He has learned how to adjust and suppress any physiological effect of hunger.

4.2   MENTAL HEALTH, HUNGER, AND POOR NUTRITION

The relationship between food insecurity and mental health issues, especially depression and anxiety, are well-researched (Messer 1989; Hamelin et al. 2002; Connell et al. 2005; Weaver and Hadley 2009; De Marco et al. 2009; Lund et al. 2010; Hadley and Crooks 2012; Wutich and Brewis 2014; Bruening et al. 2016; Maynard et al. 2018). Researchers note that uncertainty, unpredictability, and worry about how and where to get food create increased stress, which can lead to depression and anxiety (Weaver and Hadley 2009; Hadley and Crooks 2012; Wutich and Brewis 2014). Davison et al. (2017) show the relationship between food insecurity, poor nutrient intake, and mental health among Canadian adults. In their 2018 systematic review, Arenas et al. highlight the relationship between food insecurity and anxiety, reduced cognitive development in children and adults, sleep disorders, epilepsy, and depression. The authors further emphasize that the association between food insecurity and depression is strong and well-documented (Arenas et al. 2018).

Research also highlights the association between specific coping strategies and mental health issues. Some may choose to consume foods considered unclean and shameful, such as discarded or expired foods (Hamelin et al. 1999; Mintz and Du Bois 2002; Weaver and Hadley 2009; Hadley and Crooks 2012). Hadley and Crooks (2012) emphasize that the mental health struggles that accompany food insecurity may lead to decreased productivity, which impacts college students in significant ways (see Chap. 5).

4.2.1   Among College Students

National data show that mental health is a growing concern on college campuses. In the 2018 National College Health Assessment, students reported that the following mental health issues have impacted their individual academic performance: depression—18.7 percent of students (up from 13.5% in 2014), sleep difficulties—21.8 percent of students (up from 21% in 2014), stress—33.2 percent of students (up from 30.3% in 2014) (ACHA 2014, 2018).

There is a growing body of literature that shows food insecurity is associated with mental health issues on college campuses and follows similar patterns as the general population, particularly in regard to anxiety and depression (Broton et al. 2018; Bruening et al. 2016; Darling et al. 2015; Payne-Sturges et al. 2018; Hattangadi et al. 2019). Although Chap. 5 will discuss food insecurity and academic performance specifically, the context of stress and declining mental health is directly tied to academic performance, academic sacrifice, and academic motivation. For example, Martinez et al. (2018) conducted a study on the relationships between food insecurity, mental health, and academic performance in a large California public university system. Their findings show that food insecurity is related to lower academic performance (grade point average) directly and indirectly through mental health issues. Food insecurity and hunger affect one's ability to focus and concentrate on studies, which then in turn affects academic performance (Jyoti et al. 2005; Hadley and Crooks 2012; Watson et al. 2017). Bruening et al. (2016) found that freshman who experienced food insecurity had a higher rate of experiencing depression than students who were not food insecure. Similarly, Wattick et al. (2018) found that food insecurity increased the odds of both depression and anxiety among college students in Appalachia.

4.2.2   At the University of North Texas

A strong majority of food insecure students at the University of North Texas (82%) explicitly connected personal mental health issues to hunger and food insecurity. They acknowledged that being a college student is stressful, but contend that worrying about where they are going to get their next meal was an added stressor that had a major impact on their mental health. Specifically, students discussed stress (45%), depression (27%), lack of concentration/poor academics (25%), and anxiety (18%), yet these were not mutually exclusive topics. There was a considerable amount of overlap in all of these areas when students discussed mental health. Notably, in comparing students across different categories of food insecurity, students with the highest self-reported rates of mental health issues were also the most food insecure.

Ana stressed *It fills my head with other things. I am worried about food, but I should be worrying about this exam that's coming up so it kind of throws me off because I am thinking about things I shouldn't be thinking about. I have other priorities that need to be done. And because I am worrying about this other thing like food insecurity, I can't focus on everything else that needs to be done or focus on that day.* Maria is an 18-year-old Hispanic sophomore who lived on campus. She explained that the stress was too much to stay in school. She decided to take a break from school, get a job, earn some money, and then see if she could come back. *I'm not coming back next semester because I can't afford it. So, I'll either take a sabbatical or just not come back. It's really stressful.* Lynn, a 19-year-old Asian/White sophomore, highlighted how overwhelming it is to balance school and the basics of living.

> *So, feeling the weight of school stress, financial stress, food stress, was very heavy on my mind and caused a lot of stress and pressure and anxiety. It brought to light different anxieties that I think I already had and [my anxiety] was just very, very agitated by the situations. So yeah, it definitely affected me. You know, whenever you're thinking about what am I gonna do for food. I don't have much money. Wow, my engine light came on and what am I gonna do about that? You might not be directly thinking about it, but you realize that you can't even think about other things...because it's just so loud in your subconscious. You just can't focus on anything else, and it causes ... yeah, that puts a strain on your academic work, it puts a strain on your social life and your relationships. And, it's definitely, definitely something that I felt this year.*

Regina described the mental struggle and stress:

> *It's a mental struggle more than a physical struggle because you can ward off your physical tiredness by sleeping or just drinking tap water or something like that. But it starts to weigh down on you mentally after a while. It keeps repeating over and you're thinking what I'm gonna do? Should I get a job? When I get a job, I still have to pay rent and I don't really have money to pay for food and stuff like that. So, it gets tiring after a while and you just feel like maybe dropping out of school? Should I go home, or what not? I don't have any family around so it's a mental struggle. You need family support and when you don't have it, it makes me even sadder. It's like a chain reaction kind of things. I can't even eat enough to play sports and study. It's like you don't really eat, you get tired. You don't go to class and you don't do your homework like you're supposed to. Then you feel like you're letting your parents down. And then you don't really see your parents, and then you can't really pay for rent, and then it's just like, you know. It just keeps going and going. And I try to say to myself 'No, I need to stop thinking about it because all I'm just gonna do is feel like really sad and don't want to do anything.'*

Molly reflected that her depression seems to get worse when she does not have food:

> *I know I've definitely been depressed a lot lately. It kind of comes and goes. It really doesn't help whenever I don't have any food, or I don't have the money for food, so I start freaking out, and I don't like that. So yeah, it can be pretty stressful I guess, but I have to like stop and remind myself that I do have people who take me out if I need something or I can go over to their place and they will offer me food. I can go to the food pantry. I can go to the church, and I'm sure they'll do something to help me. So, I kind of try to remind myself that.*

Makayla, a 20-year-old African-American junior, explained: *I feel stranded. You know how when you're somewhere you don't want to be, but you can't really leave? That's usually how I feel. Like, when I don't have money to buy food, or I just don't have any food. It's typically how I feel. It's definitely stressful. I'd rather have somewhere to go and not have food than be at home and realize that I don't have food and just have to think about it with no solution.*

College is a stressful time for all students. However, a strong majority of food insecure students struggle with additional stress, depression, and anxiety related to finding enough food to eat so they can continue with their studies and graduate. Although not the majority, several students questioned their worthiness of being in college. In Chap. 5, I discuss further the impact of food insecurity on academic success and students' willingness to stay in college.

4.3   WHERE DOES NUTRITION FIT IN?

Above, I discussed students' reflections on how food insecurity has impacted their physical health. Nutrition emerged as a strong topic of discussion. Students knew and understood the connectedness of low calories, poor nutrition, lack of energy, getting sick, and weight issues. They also knew that they could afford only nutrient-poor foods. So, we asked participants a question to understand nutrition more deeply, "Where does nutritious food fit into this picture of hunger and food insecurity?"

Food insecure students were very direct about nutrition. *I eat to be full, not to be healthy. Health is not a priority right now. Nutritious food is hard to fit into my life right now. I have to decide between my health and my finances. It's expensive to be healthy.* The majority talked about wanting to eat healthy and prioritize nutrition, but most had issues with access, money, and time (see also Allen 2019). Students without transportation found it particularly difficult to access healthy foods. More often than not, they purchased their food from area gas stations, the corner pharmacy, or neighborhood fast-food restaurants. If a student goes into a fast-food restaurant with $5 in their pocket, they cannot afford the healthy option on the menu. They choose from the dollar menu, which is packed with items full of saturated fats that curb their immediate hunger. Caroline is a married 25-year-old White junior. She explained: *We eat a lot of pizza because usually pizza, you get the deals for five or six dollars and then that's at least two meals or three. Pizza is budget friendly. Pizza is really budget friendly. And salads are not. I don't want to pay $8 for a salad. That's a problem. Like I can buy one pizza and that's three meals.* Participants also discussed limited time to prepare cooked food. They fell back on quick, easy, convenient, and cheap food that is often nutrient-poor. This finding is consistent with a recent mixed-method study in Canada that discusses insufficient time as a major roadblock for students' ability to cook nutritious food. Students explained that demanding schedules caused them to juggle classes, work, commuting, and so forth, and slowing down to prepare food was not feasible (Hattangadi et al. 2019).

While many of the strategies to deal with food insecurity were to skip meals or eat food with low nutritional value, participants did attempt to make up for these losses in nutritional value by practicing healthy diet habits when they had the money or time to do so. Some strategies to increase the nutritional value of their food overlap with the coping strategies discussed in Chap. 2, such as planning out meals and making big pots of food to last the week. Eleven students mentioned getting nutritious food from the UNT Food Pantry. Other strategies included making special grocery trips focused on healthy foods, budgeting an extra $25 every two weeks for fruits and vegetables, watching the sale prices at stores, and only buying nutritious foods that last a long time, like almonds.

Dietary restrictions and their related expenses also played a major role in nutrition. Although 61 percent of the participants did not have any dietary restrictions, 39 percent reported restrictions that increased their struggle with affording the *right* food. Students reported being vegetarians, vegans, diabetics, having religious dietary restrictions, being international students with certain food preferences, having allergies and intolerances to specific foods, and needing reduced-sodium foods. These restrictions are not insignificant. Students often reported that they could not eat the foods served at free food events, as well as some of the food at the UNT Food Pantry.

College students were explicit in their connections between food insecurity and hunger with physical and mental health issues. They understood that cheap food is highly processed and low in nutritional value. They acknowledged that they could not afford nutritious food. This knowledge, coupled with the lack of buying power, increased their stress and anxiety. Besides increased time and money, college students would benefit from education on low-cost, nutrient-dense, and easy to prepare food.

REFERENCES

Adams, Elizabeth J., Laurence Grummer-Strawn, and Gilberto Chavez. 2003. Food Insecurity Is Associated with Increased Risk of Obesity in California Women. *The Journal of Nutrition* 133 (4): 1070–1074. https://doi.org/10.1093/jn/133.4.1070.

Alaimo, Katherine, Christine M. Olson, and Edward A. Frongillo Jr. 2002. Family Food Insufficiency, But Not Low Family Income, Is Positively Associated with Dysthymia and Suicide Symptoms in Adolescents. *The Journal of Nutrition* 132 (4): 719–725.

Allen, Alejandro C. 2019. *Study Hard, Eat Less: Exploring Food Insecurity Among College Students.* Master's Thesis, Texas State University, San Marcos, TX.

Allen, Cara Cliburn, and Nathan F. Alleman. 2019. A Private Struggle at a Private Institution: Effects of Student Hunger on Social and Academic Experiences. *Journal of College Student Development* 60 (1): 52–69. https://doi.org/10.1353/csd.2019.0003.

American College Health Association (ACHA). 2014. *National College Health Assessment: Spring 2014 Reference Group Executive Summary.* https://www.acha.org/documents/ncha/ACHA-NCHA-II_ReferenceGroup_ExecutiveSummary_Spring2014.pdf. Accessed 11 April 2019.

———. 2018. *National College Health Assessment: Spring 2018 Reference Group Executive Summary.* https://www.acha.org/documents/ncha/NCHA-II_Spring_2018_Reference_Group_Executive_Summary.pdf.   Accessed 15 May 2019.

Arenas, Daniel Jose, Sara Zhou, Arthur Thomas, Jici Wang, Gilberto Vila Arroyo, and Katie Bash. 2018. Negative Health Outcomes Associated with Food Insecurity Status in the United States of America: A Systematic Review of Peer-reviewed Studies. *NutriXiv*, September 11. https://doi.org/10.31232/osf.io/uk9xw.

Ashe, Leah M., and Roberta Sonnino. 2013. At the Crossroads: New Paradigms of Food Security, Public Health Nutrition and School Food. *Public Health Nutrition* 16 (6): 1020–1027. https://doi.org/10.1017/s1368980012004326.

Basiotis, P.P., and M. Lino. 2002. Food Insufficiency and Prevalence of Overweight Among Adult Women. *Family Economics and Nutrition Review* 15: 55.

Broton, Katharine, Kari Weaver, and Minhtuyen Mai. 2018. Hunger in Higher Education: Experiences and Correlates of Food Insecurity Among Wisconsin Undergraduates from Low-Income Families. *Social Sciences* 7 (10): 179. https://doi.org/10.3390/socsci7100179.

Bruening, Meg, Stephanie Brennhofer, Irene Van Woerden, Michael Todd, and Melissa Laska. 2016. Factors Related to the High Rates of Food Insecurity Among Diverse, Urban College Freshmen. *Journal of the Academy of Nutrition and Dietetics* 116 (9): 1450–1457. https://doi.org/10.1016/j.jand.2016.04.004.

Bruening, Meg, Irene Van Woerden, Michael Todd, and Melissa N. Laska. 2018. Hungry to Learn: The Prevalence and Effects of Food Insecurity on Health Behaviors and Outcomes Over Time Among a Diverse Sample of University Freshmen. *International Journal of Behavioral Nutrition and Physical Activity* 15 (1). https://doi.org/10.1186/s12966-018-0647-7.

Burris, Mecca, Sarah Bradley, David Himmelgreen, Kayla Rykiel, Paige Tucker, Danielle Hintz, and Elisa Shannon. 2018. Teen Food Insecurity in Pinellas County Technical Report, May 19. https://www.jwbpinellas.org/wp-content/uploads/2018/06/Teen-food-insecurity-in-Pinellas-County_Technical-Report_5-21-2018.pdf. Accessed 17 May 2019.

Casey, Patrick, Susan Goolsby, Carol Berkowitz, Deborah Frank, John Cook, Diana Cutts, Maureen M. Black, Nieves Zaldivar, Suzette Levenson, Tim Heeren, Alan Meyers, and the Children's Sentinel Nutrition Assessment Program Study Group. 2004. Maternal Depression, Changing Public Assistance, Food Security, and Child Health Status. *Pediatrics* 113 (2): 298–304.

Chilton, M., J.M. Chyatte, and J. Breaux. 2007. The Negative Effects of Poverty & Food Insecurity on Child Development. *Indian Journal of Medical Research* 126 (4): 262–272.

Coleman-Jensen, Alisha, Mark Nord, Margaret Andrews, and Steven Carlson. 2012. *Household Food Security in the United States in 2011.* Report No. 141. Department of Agriculture, Economic Research Service.

Connell, Carol L., Kristi L. Lofton, Kathy Yadrick, and Timothy A. Rehner. 2005. Children's Experiences of Food Insecurity Can Assist in Understanding Its Effect on Their Well-Being. *The Journal of Nutrition* 135 (7): 1683–1690. https://doi.org/10.1093/jn/135.7.1683.

Darling, Katherine E., Amy J. Fahrenkamp, Shana M. Wilson, Alexandra L. D'Auria, and Amy F. Sato. 2015. Physical and Mental Health Outcomes

Associated with Prior Food Insecurity Among Young Adults. *Journal of Health Psychology* 22 (5): 572–581. https://doi.org/10.1177/1359105315609087.

Darmon, Nicole, André Briend, and Adam Drewnowski. 2004. Energy-dense Diets Are Associated with Lower Diet Costs: A Community Study of French Adults. *Public Health Nutrition* 7 (1): 21–27. https://doi.org/10.1079/phn2003512.

Davison, Karen, Lovedeep Gondara, and Bonnie Kaplan. 2017. Food Insecurity, Poor Diet Quality, and Suboptimal Intakes of Folate and Iron Are Independently Associated with Perceived Mental Health in Canadian Adults. *Nutrients* 9 (3): 274. https://doi.org/10.3390/nu9030274.

De Marco, M., S. Thorburn, and J. Due. 2009. In a Country as Affluent as America, People Should Be Eating: Experiences with and Perceptions of Food Insecurity among Rural and Urban Oregonians. *Qualitative Health Research* 19 (7): 1010–1024. https://doi.org/10.1177/1049732309338868.

Dhillon, Jaapna, L. Karina Diaz Rios, Kaitlyn Aldaz, Natalie De La Cruz, Emily Vu, Syed Asad Asghar, Quintin Kuse, and Rudy Ortiz. 2019. We Don't Have a Lot of Healthy Options: Food Environment Perceptions of First-Year, Minority College Students Attending a Food Desert Campus. *Nutrients* 11 (4): 816. https://doi.org/10.3390/nu11040816.

Dietz, William H. 1995. Does Hunger Cause Obesity? *Pediatrics* 95: 766–767. https://doi.org/10.3390/nu11040816.

Dinour, Lauren M., Dara Bergen, and Ming-Chin Yeh. 2007. The Food Insecurity–Obesity Paradox: A Review of the Literature and the Role Food Stamps May Play. *Journal of the American Dietetic Association* 107 (11): 1952–1961. https://doi.org/10.1016/j.jada.2007.08.006.

Farahbakhsh, Jasmine, Mahitab Hanbazaza, Geoff D.C. Ball, Anna P. Farmer, Katerina Maximova, and Noreen D. Willows. 2017. Food Insecure Student Clients of a University-based Food Bank Have Compromised Health, Dietary Intake and Academic Quality. *Nutrition & Dietetics* 74 (1): 67–73. https://doi.org/10.1111/1747-0080.12307.

Finney Rutten, Lila J., Amy L. Yaroch, Uriyoan Colón-Ramos, Wendy Johnson-Askew, and Mary Story. 2010. Poverty, Food Insecurity, and Obesity: A Conceptual Framework for Research, Practice, and Policy. *Journal of Hunger & Environmental Nutrition* 5: 403–415. https://doi.org/10.1080/1932024 8.2010.527275.

Fram, Maryah Stella, Lorrene D. Ritchie, Nila Rosen, and Edward A. Frongillo. 2015. Child Experience of Food Insecurity Is Associated with Child Diet and Physical Activity. *The Journal of Nutrition* 145 (3): 499–504. https://doi.org/10.3945/jn.114.194365.

Frank, Deborah A., Patrick H. Casey, Maureen M. Black, Ruth Rose Jacobs, Mariana Chilton, Diana Cutts, Elizabeth March, Timothy Heeren, Sharon Coleman, Stephanie Ettinger de Cuba, and John T. Cook. 2010. Cumulative

Hardship and Wellness of Low-Income, Young Children: Multisite Surveillance Study. *Pediatrics* 125 (5): e1115–e1123.

Franklin, Brandi, Ashley Jones, Dejuan Love, Stephane Puckett, Justin Macklin, and Shelley White-Means. 2012. Exploring Mediators of Food Insecurity and Obesity: A Review of Recent Literature. *Journal of Community Health* 37 (1): 253–264. https://doi.org/10.1007/s10900-011-9420-4.

Garner, A.S., J.P. Shonkoff, B.S. Siegel, M.I. Dobbins, M.F. Earls, A.S. Garner, L. Mcguinn, J. Pascoe, and D.L. Wood. 2012. Early Childhood Adversity, Toxic Stress, and the Role of the Pediatrician: Translating Developmental Science into Lifelong Health. *Pediatrics* 129 (1). https://doi.org/10.1542/peds.2011-2662.

Greene, Lamar. 2018. *The Effects of Childhood Food Insecurity. Destination Health EU: The Center for the Study of Human Health Blog*, March 29. //www.destinationhealtheu.org/news-perspectives/the-effectsof-childhood-food-insecurity. Accessed 1 May 2019.

Hadley, Craig, and Deborah L. Crooks. 2012. Coping and the Biosocial Consequences of Food Insecurity in the 21st Century. *American Journal of Physical Anthropology* 149 (S55): 72–94. https://doi.org/10.1002/ajpa.22161.

Hamelin, Anne-Marie, Jean-Pierre Habicht, and Micheline Beaudry. 1999. Food Insecurity: Consequences for the Household and Broader Social Implications. *The Journal of Nutrition* 129 (2): 525S–528S. https://doi.org/10.1093/jn/129.2.525s.

Hamelin, Anne-Marie, Micheline Beaudry, and Jean-Pierre Habicht. 2002. Characterization of Household Food Insecurity in Québec: Food and Feelings. *Social Science & Medicine* 54 (1): 119–132. https://doi.org/10.1016/s0277-9536(01)00013-2.

Hamrick, Karen S., and Ket McClelland. 2016. *Americans Eating Patterns and Time Spent on Food: The 2014 Eating & Health Module Data*. Report No. 158. United States Department of Agriculture, July. https://pdfs.semanticscholar.org/f71d/fb4a9c9a9d7b12d9acd83544a554550c0d08.pdf.

Hattangadi, Nayantara, Ellen Vogel, Linda Carroll, and Pierre Côté. 2019. "Everybody I Know Is Always Hungry…But Nobody Asks Why": University Students, Food Insecurity and Mental Health. *Sustainability* 11 (6): 1571. https://doi.org/10.3390/su11061571.

Henry, Lisa. 2017. Understanding Food Insecurity Among College Students: Experience, Motivation, and Local Solutions. *Annals of Anthropological Practice* 41 (1): 6–19. https://doi.org/10.1111/napa.12108.

Higashi, Robin T., Simon J. Craddock Lee, Tammy Leonard, Erica L. Cuate, Jay Cole, and Sandi L. Pruitt. 2015. Multiple Comorbidities and Interest in Research Participation among Clients of a Nonprofit Food Distribution Site. *Clinical and Translational Science* 8 (5): 584–590. https://doi.org/10.1111/cts.12325.

Himmelgreen, David. 2013. Using a Life Course Approach and a Bio-cultural Perspective to Understand the Food Insecurity and Obesity Paradox. *Cadernos De Saúde Pública* 29 (2). https://doi.org/10.1590/s0102-311x2013000200006.

Himmelgreen, David, Rafael Pérez-Escamilla, Sofia Segura-Millan, Yu-Kuei Peng, Anir Gonzalez, Merrill Singer, and Ann Ferris. 2000. Food Insecurity Among Low-Income Hispanics in Hartford, Connecticut: Implications for Public Health Policy. *Human Organization* 59 (3): 334–342. https://doi.org/10.17730/humo.59.3.76557m3177481414.

Hughes, Roger, Irene Serebryanikova, Katherine Donaldson, and Michael Leveritt. 2011. Student Food Insecurity: The Skeleton in the University Closet. *Nutrition & Dietetics* 68 (1): 27–32. https://doi.org/10.1111/j.1747-0080.2010.01496.x.

Ivers, Louise C., and Kimberly A. Cullen. 2011. Food Insecurity: Special Considerations for Women. *The American Journal of Clinical Nutrition* 94 (6): 1740S–1744S. https://doi.org/10.3945/ajcn.111.012617.

Jyoti, Diana F., Edward A. Frongillo, and Sonya J. Jones. 2005. Food Insecurity Affects School Childrens Academic Performance, Weight Gain, and Social Skills. *The Journal of Nutrition* 135 (12): 2831–2839. https://doi.org/10.1093/jn/135.12.2831.

Kirkpatrick, Sharon I., and Valerie Tarasuk. 2008. Food Insecurity Is Associated with Nutrient Inadequacies among Canadian Adults and Adolescents. *The Journal of Nutrition* 138 (3): 604–612. https://doi.org/10.1093/jn/138.3.604.

Knol, Linda L., Cliff A. Robb, Erin M. Mckinley, and Mary Wood. 2017. Food Insecurity, Self-Rated Health, and Obesity Among College Students. *American Journal of Health Education* 48 (4): 248–255. https://doi.org/10.1080/19325037.2017.1316689.

Knowles, Molly, Jenny Rabinowich, Tianna Gaines-Turner, and Mariana Chilton. 2015. Witnesses to Hunger: Methods for Photovoice and Participatory Action Research in Public Health. *Human Organization* 74 (3): 255–265.

Laraia, B.A. 2013. Food Insecurity and Chronic Disease. *Advances in Nutrition* 4 (2): 203–212. https://doi.org/10.3945/an.112.003277.

Leung, Cindy W., Elissa S. Epel, Lorrene D. Ritchie, Patricia B. Crawford, and Barbara A. Laraia. 2014. Food Insecurity Is Inversely Associated with Diet Quality of Lower-Income Adults. *Journal of the Academy of Nutrition and Dietetics* 114 (12): 1943–1953. https://doi.org/10.1016/j.jand.2014.06.353.

Lund, Crick, Alison Breen, Alan J. Flisher, Ritsuko Kakuma, Joanne Corrigall, John A. Joska, Leslie Swartz, and Vikram Patel. 2010. Poverty and Common Mental Disorders in Low and Middle Income Countries: A Systematic Review. *Social Science & Medicine* 71 (3): 517–528. https://doi.org/10.1016/j.socscimed.2010.04.027.

Martinez, Suzanna M., Edward A. Frongillo, Cindy Leung, and Lorrene Ritchie. 2018. No Food for Thought: Food Insecurity Is Related to Poor Mental Health and Lower Academic Performance among Students in California's Public University System. *Journal of Health Psychology*, 135910531878302, June 1. https://doi.org/10.1177/1359105318783028.

Maynard, Merryn, Lesley Andrade, Sara Packull-Mccormick, Christopher Perlman, Cesar Leos-Toro, and Sharon Kirkpatrick. 2018. Food Insecurity and Mental Health Among Females in High-Income Countries. *International Journal of Environmental Research and Public Health* 15 (7): E1424. https://doi.org/10.3390/ijerph15071424.

Messer, Ellen. 1989. Seasonal Hunger and Coping Strategies: An Anthropological Discussion. In *Coping with Seasonal Constraints*. Philadelphia, PA: University Museum, University of Pennsylvania.

Meza, Anthony, Emily Altman, Suzanna Martinez, and Cindy W. Leung. 2018. "It's a Feeling That One Is Not Worth Food": A Qualitative Study Exploring the Psychosocial Experience and Academic Consequences of Food Insecurity Among College Students. *Journal of the Academy of Nutrition and Dietetics*, December 12. https://doi.org/10.1016/j.jand.2018.09.006.

Mintz, Sidney Winfried, and Christine M. Du Bois. 2002. The Anthropology of Food and Eating. *Annual Review of Anthropology* 31: 99–119. https://doi.org/10.1146/annurev.anthro.32.032702.131011.

Mirabitur, Erica, Karen E. Peterson, Colleen Rathz, Stacey Matlen, and Nicole Kasper. 2016. Predictors of College-Student Food Security and Fruit and Vegetable Intake Differ by Housing Type. *Journal of American College Health* 64 (7): 555–564. https://doi.org/10.1080/07448481.2016.1192543.

Olson, Christine M. 1999. Nutrition and Health Outcomes Associated with Food Insecurity and Hunger. *The Journal of Nutrition* 129 (2): 521S–524S. https://doi.org/10.1093/jn/129.2.521s.

Patton-López, Megan M., Daniel F. López-Cevallos, Doris I. Cancel-Tirado, and Leticia Vazquez. 2014. Prevalence and Correlates of Food Insecurity among Students Attending a Midsize Rural University in Oregon. *Journal of Nutrition Education and Behavior* 46 (3): 209–214. https://doi.org/10.1016/j.jneb.2013.10.007.

Payne-Sturges, Devon C., Allison Tjaden, Kimberly M. Caldeira, Kathryn B. Vincent, and Amelia M. Arria. 2018. Student Hunger on Campus: Food Insecurity Among College Students and Implications for Academic Institutions. *American Journal of Health Promotion* 32 (2): 349–354. https://doi.org/10.1177/0890117117719620.

Quandt, Sara, and Pamela Rao. 1999. Hunger and Food Security Among Older Adults in a Rural Community. *Human Organization* 58 (1): 28–35. https://doi.org/10.17730/humo.58.1.q28k2506ur45215h.

Rose-Jacobs, Ruth, Maureen M. Black, Patrick H. Casey, John T. Cook, Diana B. Cutts, Mariana Chilton, Timothy Heeren, Suzette M. Levenson, Alan F. Meyers, and Deborah A. Frank. 2008. Household Food Insecurity: Associations with At-Risk Infant and Toddler Development. *Pediatrics* 121 (1): 65–72. https://doi.org/10.1542/peds.2006-3717.

Seligman, Hilary K., Barbara A. Laraia, and Margot B. Kushel. 2010. Food Insecurity Is Associated with Chronic Disease Among Low-Income NHANES Participants. *The Journal of Nutrition* 140 (2): 304–310. https://doi.org/10.3945/jn.109.112573.

Townsend, Marilyn S., Janet Peerson, Bradley Love, Cheryl Achterberg, and Suzanne P. Murphy. 2001. Food Insecurity Is Positively Related to Overweight in Women. *The Journal of Nutrition* 131 (6): 1738–1745. https://doi.org/10.1093/jn/131.6.1738.

Watson, Tyler D., Hannah Malan, Deborah Glik, and Suzanna M. Martinez. 2017. College Students Identify University Support for Basic Needs and Life Skills as Key Ingredient in Addressing Food Insecurity on Campus. *California Agriculture* 71 (3): 130–138. https://doi.org/10.3733/ca.2017a0023.

Wattick, Rachel, Rebecca Hagedorn, and Melissa Olfert. 2018. Relationship Between Diet and Mental Health in a Young Adult Appalachian College Population. *Nutrients* 10 (8): 957. https://doi.org/10.3390/nu10080957.

Weaver, Lesley Jo, and Connor B. Fasel. 2018. A Systematic Review of the Literature on the Relationships between Chronic Diseases and Food Insecurity. *Food and Nutrition Sciences* 9: 519–541. https://doi.org/10.4236/fns.2018.95040.

Weaver, Lesley Jo, and Craig Hadley. 2009. Moving Beyond Hunger and Nutrition: A Systematic Review of the Evidence Linking Food Insecurity and Mental Health in Developing Countries. *Ecology of Food and Nutrition* 48 (4): 263–284. https://doi.org/10.1080/03670240903001167.

Weinstein, James L., Katie S. Martin, and Ann M. Ferris. 2009. Household Food Security Varies Within Month and Is Related to Childhood Anemia. *Journal of Hunger & Environmental Nutrition* 4 (1): 48–61. https://doi.org/10.1080/19320240802706833.

Whitaker, R.C., S.M. Phillips, and S.M. Orzol. 2006. Food Insecurity and the Risks of Depression and Anxiety in Mothers and Behavior Problems in Their Preschool-Aged Children. *Pediatrics* 118 (3): E859–E568. https://doi.org/10.1542/peds.2006-0239.

Wutich, Amber, and Alexandra Brewis. 2014. Food, Water, and Scarcity: Toward a Broader Anthropology of Resource Insecurity. *Current Anthropology* 55 (4): 444–468. https://doi.org/10.1086/677311.

CHAPTER 5

Academic Success and Motivation

Abstract This chapter begins with a literature review on food insecurity and academic success among K-12 students, followed by a discussion of the expanding research on college students. Interview participants were asked if food insecurity has impacted their student success or performance in a course. This chapter shows the grit needed to be academically success-ful despite food insecurity. I discuss specific academic sacrifices in order to have more money for food, followed by a discussion of any activities, in class or extra-curricular, that were avoided because of issues with food insecurity. The final section discusses what motivates students to stay in college while they are food insecure.

Keywords Food insecurity • Academic success • Academic sacrifices • Motivation

> *My success is greater than me. The plans that I have established to be successful are greater than a little temporary hunger.* (Tyron, 19-year-old, African-American, freshman, on campus)

Food insecure students are tremendously motivated to finish college and move on from what they see as a temporary food insecurity situation. This chapter shows the commitment, dedication, and sacrifice of students in order to be academically successful in college despite food insecurity.

© The Author(s) 2020
L. Henry, *Experiences of Hunger and Food Insecurity in College,*
https://doi.org/10.1007/978-3-030-31818-5_5

Sophia is a 22-year-old junior. Her family migrated to the U.S. when she was 12 years old. She explained that she grew up in a poor family but was never hungry and never lacked food. She received free breakfast and lunch at school, but did not remember a time in her life when she was without access to food. That changed when she came to college. She transferred to UNT during her sophomore year after taking classes at a local community college. She had a federal grant, a UNT scholarship, and loan money that covered her tuition and some of her rent. Sophia moved out of her parents' house to come to UNT, and was proud to have an apartment. It was also expensive. She realized that working a part-time job was not providing enough money to cover all the expenses. She began to eat less and less. She sometimes swiped her friend's meal plan ID in the school cafeterias, which she knew was against the rules. She found the UNT Food Pantry. But her grades were suffering: *The teacher would ask 'why didn't you guys pass this? I literally said all this in class.' And I'm like 'I don't remember none of that. Cause I can't concentrate in class.'* She was on academic suspension at the time of the interview and needed to get her grades up to keep her scholarship. She did not want to give up on college. She explained:

> *Because I know that soon as I graduate, I can pay my loans off. I want to be a pediatric physical therapist, and I want to be in the grad track program for it so I have to have a certain GPA, a 3.0. Some people give up. My mom, she didn't graduate from college. My dad didn't graduate from college. My sister just graduated, and I'm the second child. What would it look like for me not to graduate from college? Plus, after I graduate, I want to go to Paris. I want to do so much stuff in my life, and I can't do that if I don't finish these proper steps in my life. Somebody told me when I was 17 that the first 20 years of your life will determine the next 20 years.*

The relationship between food insecurity and academic performance is not well understood at the college level. However, it is well-documented that food insecurity in children has a negative impact on cognitive skills and behavioral issues (Kleinman et al. 1998; Murphy et al. 1998; Reid 2000; Alaimo et al. 2001; Jyoti et al. 2005; Shankar et al. 2017). As Jyoti et al. (2005) note, students need nutritious food to thrive, not just live. The pipeline approach (Cole and Barber 2003; Hinton et al. 2010) suggests that if food insecurity is detrimental to K-12 student success, then it is also detrimental to the success of college students. It is difficult to concentrate when hunger and worry about your next meal consume your thoughts. Fortunately, the research on how food insecurity impacts academic success in college has been rapidly advancing in the past five years.

University administrators concerned with graduation and retention rates should understand that food insecurity is a threat and barrier to academic success. Recent studies show that food insecurity in college is associated with lower grade point averages (GPAs) (Patton-López et al. 2014; Maroto et al. 2015; Martinez et al. 2016; Morris et al. 2016; El Zein et al. 2017; McArthur et al. 2018; O'Neill and Maguire 2017; Payne-Sturges et al. 2018; Phillips et al. 2018; Simon et al. 2018; van Woerden et al. 2018; Wooten et al. 2018; Camelo and Elliott 2019; El Zein et al. 2019; Goldrick-Rab et al. 2019; Weaver et al. 2019). Maroto et al. (2015) conducted one of the earliest studies investigating the relationship between food insecurity and student grade point average. They reported that food insecure students were more likely than food secure students to report a low GPA (2.0–2.49). Phillips et al. (2018) conducted a study in a large urban public university in the Midwest. Their results show, compared to food secure students, students with food insecurity experiences were 3.49 times more likely to consider dropping out of college, 3.58 times more likely to reduce their course load, and 3.42 times more likely to neglect their academic studies. Food insecurity was also associated with lower GPAs. van Woerden et al. (2018) found that food insecure first-year students at a large, public university had a slightly lower average GPA than food secure students, when high school academic performance was controlled. In a study among undergraduates at a midsize New Jersey public university, Weaver et al. (2019) tested the odds of food insecure students either underachieving (falling in the bottom ten percent of GPA) or overachieving (falling in the top ten percent of GPA). Their results showed that food insecure students were two times as likely to be in the lowest ten percent of GPA and three times less likely to be in the top ten percent of GPA compared to food secure students. Wooten et al. (2018) noted that compared to students with higher GPAs, students with GPAs below 3.0 were 2.9 times more likely to experience food insecurity. From a 2019 national survey of 86,000 students, Goldrick-Rab et al. (2019) report that students experiencing food insecurity had a lower GPA than those not experiencing food insecurity.

As will be discussed below, GPA is not the only measure that indicates academic success is suffering among those who experience food insecurity. Other researchers examine the nuances of how food insecurity impacts

academic behaviors and academic achievement, including time to graduation and retention (Silva et al. 2015; Hagedorn and Olfert 2018; McArthur
et al. 2018; Payne-Sturges et al. 2018). Silva et al. (2015) found that food
insecure college students are more likely to have failed and withdrawn
from courses. Hagedorn and Olfert (2018) conducted a study in a large
central Appalachian university. They assessed academic performance by
asking students to rate their progress in school, time to graduation, class
attendance, class attention, and understanding the course content. Their
results were consistent with other studies that show food insecure students
reporting lower academic performance, as well as lower GPAs. McArthur
et al. (2018) show that when compared to food secure students, food
insecure students scored lower on overall progress in school, class attendance, attention span in class, and understanding concepts taught in class.
Allen and Alleman (2019) report that students at Status U made academic
sacrifices by not being able to study, making choices between food and
books, quitting activities (like the opera) in order to pick up additional
work shifts, and even taking off semesters to work. Payne-Sturges et al.
(2018) call for additional studies that examine "delayed graduation, dis-
continuous enrollment, and attenuation of academic goals as possible consequences of food insecurity" (2018, 352).

Many compounding factors contribute to reduced academic success
among those who experience food insecurity in college, and scholars are
calling for continued research to better understand the complexity. As
noted in Chap. 4, research shows that stress, anxiety, and declining mental
health related to limited financial resources and food insecurity are related
to academic performance and success (Patton- López et al. 2014; Maroto
et al. 2015; Morris et al. 2016; Farahbakhsh et al. 2017; O'Neill and
Maguire 2017; Payne-Sturges et al. 2018; Watson et al. 2017; Eisenberg
et al. 2016; Martinez et al. 2018; Meza et al. 2018; van Woerden et al.
2018; El Zein et al. 2019; Weaver et al. 2019). Patton-López et al. (2014)
note that food insecure students are more likely to work, which limits time
available for studying. Several studies specifically identify stress as a vari-
able leading to the inability to concentrate and reduced academic performance (Eisenberg et al. 2016; Payne-Sturges et al. 2018; van Woerden
et al. 2018; Meza et al. 2018). Payne-Sturges et al. found that food insecure students "reported more frequent depression symptoms (little
interest, feeling down, feeling tired, poor appetite, and feeling bad about
oneself) and that they experienced disruptions in academic work as a result
of depression symptoms" (2018, 350; see also Patton- López et al. 2014;

Watson et al. 2017; Martinez et al. 2018). Other studies identify low energy and the inability to concentrate as factors contributing to trouble concentrating in class and while studying, as well as lower academic performance (Farahbakhsh et al. 2017; O'Neill and Maguire 2017; Weaver et al. 2019). Meza et al. (2018) report that students lack energy, sleep a great deal, and focus more time thinking about food than on academics. All of this impacts their performance in school.

5.1   At the University of North Texas

Interview participants were asked a series of open-ended, qualitative questions related to how food insecurity impacted academic success, performance in a course, and school activities; specific academic sacrifices; and what motivated them to continue with school.

5.1.1   Academic Success

As discussed in the previous chapter, students recognized a relationship between food insecurity, low energy, and lack of concentration. When asked if food insecurity had impacted their student success in any way, 76 percent said yes, primarily through low energy levels, shakiness, lack of ability to concentrate, and lack of ability to get out of bed. Specifically, some discussed that hunger made studying hard or impossible, made them feel shaky and faint in class, and generally made it difficult to focus or concentrate during class. Others focused on their low energy and how it was difficult to participate in class. Several students stated that they were so drained of energy during periods of extreme food insecurity that they were unable to get up in the morning to attend class. Still others commented that the stress of being food insecure affected their performance and concentration both while studying and in class. Jayla is an 18-year-old African-American freshman who lived on campus. She described her experience in class:

I was hungry. I was like starving. My stomach was growling and everything. I couldn't pay attention because I was hungry. I was so hungry, and I needed to eat. The professor was talking, and I was at the front row, and I felt so much tension and embarrassment. Because I was on the front row, and I was not paying attention. His focus was on me, and he ended up calling me out because of it. I was not paying attention like I should have been because I hadn't eaten, but he didn't know I hadn't eaten.

Melissa, a 34-year-old White junior, explained: *On days when I haven't had anything to eat, I'm nodding off at the computer trying to read 20 pages. It's hard. It's really difficult. As much as I push myself through, I know that I can only do so much until I need to eat again. I get headaches if I don't eat, tired, cranky. Just feeling like bland. It's a lot harder to learn.* Makayla is a 20-year-old African-American junior. She told of her experience: *I literally could not concentrate. I really wanted to concentrate, but I really couldn't get out of my bed and study. Therefore, I made a really bad grade, like the worst grade I've ever made in college history. I retook it (later) and I got an A.* Erika, a 19-year-old White freshman who lived on campus, explained the complicatedness of her concentration:

> *I wasn't really able to concentrate on anything for longer than a short while. The classroom was a little better than at home, because I had strategies to keep up with it. I'd splash water on my face. I'd get up to go to the bathroom a few times and just keep myself awake, keep myself concentrating. In my Stats class, I could not concentrate longer than 3 or 4 words. He had a really monotone voice, and I couldn't concentrate very long. I skipped class quite a bit just so that I could sleep because I couldn't stay awake.*

Regina, a 19-year-old African-American sophomore, added: *So, I guess, as long as I eat good enough, I can focus for the whole day. I bring my food up here and stuff like that to snack on. And if not, I just start to get drowsy and I don't really pay attention. My mind is just like, hazy, 'cuz it just wants to shuts down, 'cuz it doesn't have enough nutrition. So, yeah.*

Participants (23%) reported that food insecurity impacted their academic success because of time management issues. Some students said that they were too busy studying to remember to eat, while others said that by the end of the day, they were too tired to both study and eat. A few students also commented on their own lack of foresight in scheduling their days. They did not schedule themselves time to eat during their school day and then were hungry and unable to concentrate in class. Many students discussed the option of dropping courses in order to work more hours at their jobs. They saw earning more money as a solution to maintaining their apartment, having enough money for food, and keeping up with their remaining classes. Molly, a 19-year-old White freshman who lived in the dorms, shared her experience: *I had to go down to nine credit hours just because I have to work more, so I can feed myself. I can't afford a full meal plan. I don't have enough money to eat on the weekends. So that's affected my college career, for sure. I had to limit my hours.* Ashley is also a 19-year-old White freshman who lived in the dorms. She shared her decision-making process:

> *I was majorly depressed last semester and really stressed out because I was filling up my entire weekend with friends and my club activities. I work, and I took fifteen hours. So, I just made a list. I was like okay, I've got to either drop a class, drop all my weekend activities, or drop my job. And I was really considering dropping my job. I was waffling again—do I want to drop a class and have to go to school longer? It was pretty much—I have to either drop a class, have to go to school longer, pay more money in the long run, or drop my friends and only worry about work and school, which is not fun. I mean, I could have gone to community college if I wanted not to have the college experience and not hang out with new people. Or else I could drop my job, which means not saving at all for next year and be really stretching my dollars. So, I just dropped a class. So yeah, I had to drop a class because I needed to keep my job for next year.*

Students who dropped courses face additional concerns, such as reduced financial aid and a longer time to graduation, but they explained that working more hours and making more money was a way to put food on their tables.

5.1.2   School Sacrifices

Participants were asked to discuss specific academic sacrifices in order to have more money for food. Fifty-one percent of participants made some form of academic sacrifice in order to eat. These sacrifices most often included not purchasing textbooks and missing class in order to work. Students said that they would either wait to see if the textbooks were really necessary or else they would not buy them altogether. Arush, a 22-year-old international South Asian senior, explained: *Basically, our textbooks, they cost a lot. They're like $300–$400 dollars. And that's a lot. I can't pay $300 for a textbook. I could pay for my one month living expenses with that. So, I would rather pay for my living expenses than buy this textbook because my professor teaches the same stuff and she also gives us the presentations in PowerPoint slides.* The issue of students not buying textbooks because they are too expensive is not always related to food insecurity. Professors are aware that many students do not purchase the necessary textbooks. At the same time, it is important for university administrators to understand that some students are making significant academic sacrifices in order to eat.

Participants also discussed skipping class or other class activities in order to make money. Some students with steady work were asked to pick up extra shifts during their class time and found it difficult to say no because they needed the money. Other students noted the need to meet clients during class time. Students without transportation discussed missing class because they could only get rides to work by friends during their class time. Michael is a 21-year-old Asian/White junior who explained: *I skipped a couple classes once. Well, not once, but a couple times to take a shift for money, but I don't really do that a lot. I do it maybe twice a semester. It was for a [3-hour] night class that wasn't really important. He had all his stuff on PowerPoint, so I just decided I was gonna skip it those times.* Participants who skipped class to earn money for food related feelings of guilt over missing the school work.

Of those participants who discussed academic sacrifices, 71 percent had experiences with food insecurity as children. There are a few reasons considered for this pattern. Students who have experience with long-term food insecurity may be more willing to compromise their academic standing due to fear of malnourishment. They may be willing to make a few non-threatening academic sacrifices now in order to balance school and livelihood for future long-term academic success.

5.1.3   School Activities

Students were asked if any activities, in class or extra-curricular, were avoided because of issues with food insecurity. Fifty-five percent of participants stated that they have no barrier to participation due to food insecurity. Rather, many of these students attended certain school activities because of the university's benevolence to students. One participant noted: *I mean, I usually go to campus activities <u>because</u> there's food.* For students who discussed about not participating in activities, reasons given included an inability to pay dues and the need to work. Participants stated that they were unable to join Greek organizations, honor societies, and some academic clubs because of the membership fees. Other students said they were too busy working to attend activities. Allen and Alleman (2019) note that food insecure students at Status U also wrestled with involvement in school activities. Many struggled with juggling class, work, and organizations/athletic events. Some attended events because of the free food. Others reported that events were very expensive, but it was important to attend for their sense of belonging with campus life.

5.1.4   *Motivations*

With all of the struggles—the hunger, the poor nutrition, the lack of energy, the difficulty concentrating, the stress, depression, and anxiety, the juggling of work and class time—what motivates food insecure students to stay in college? After discussing how their academic success had been impacted by food insecurity and the sacrifices they made, participants were asked what motivates them to keep going and stay in school while they are food insecure. They spoke about their motivations to attend college and their motivations to stay in college. They acknowledged that staying in school despite food insecurity and other stressors took priority over hunger and health (see also Allen and Alleman 2019). Their motivations included: college as a step toward financial security, setting goals and following through, family expectations, and the contention that food insecurity is only temporary.

The strongest motivation (36%) to stay in college despite being food insecure was that a college degree is seen as a step toward financial security. This theme was highlighted in Chap. 1 when discussing the shift in the demographic profile of undergraduate college students and the subsequent rise in national rates of food insecure college students (Hughes et al. 2011; Hout 2012; Carnevale et al. 2014; Goldrick-Rab 2016; Ma et al. 2016). Participants stated that they have career goals, and they did not want to remain in low-income and hourly jobs forever. They knew a college degree would eventually lead them to a better paycheck and a better life. Brad is a 25-year-old White junior. He described the pivotal and shocking moment that contributed to his motivation to stay in college: *My girlfriend was pregnant with my child. She even gave me a sonogram picture. And then she had an abortion due to the fact that I was not financially secure. That's what she told me. So, at that point in time, I realized that it would be of greatest concern to try to obtain the means to be able to take care of a child.* Danielle, a 20-year-old White junior, explained:

> *I'm the first person to go to college in my family. On my dad's and mom's side. So, I feel like you always hear about the poverty cycle, and how you're always in it. If you're born into it, you're gonna be living in poverty. So, I think that's always something I keep in mind. I want to break it. I don't want to live like that. My mom had to live like that when she grew up. My brother and I had to too. I just, I don't like it, and I don't want my kids to do that.*

Melissa, a 34-year-old White junior, stated:

I've got to keep going no matter what. I've got to make this work because to me, it's my life. This is the way I will never be hungry again once I graduate. Years ago, I was only capable of getting entry level jobs or food service jobs with my high school diploma. I have to remember those times. That is my life force right here. I've got to complete this. I've got to keep going because there's going to be a time that I'm going to get a degree. And once I get that degree, there should be no reason for me to be hungry again because I will be able to get a better job. And like I said, a better job equals better food.

Joel, a 29-year-old White junior, discussed his goals in comparison to his roommate's experience:

I could work a job and make minimum wage. But like, what's the point of that working minimum wage job? Right now, in this day and age, it doesn't get you very far in life. I want to own a house and be able to go places. Have fun. And I know I can't do that working just an hourly job. I have a roommate who isn't in school right now, and he works every day at CVS. Eight hours a day. Fridays, he works at Sonic. It's great. It's great for him right now. But he doesn't necessarily enjoy that job. He likes living with us now, but he doesn't want to live with us his whole life. It's great for now, but like, I don't see any point in wasting my time that way. I would rather be in school than waste my time making an extra dollar.

Another motivation to stay in school was being a passionate or driven person who sets goals and follows through with them (15%) (see also Allen 2019). Many of these students were aspiring to reach their chosen profession. "I've always wanted to be a teacher" explained one student about his passion. Faith in one's own ability to succeed may be an important asset for students who face challenges of food insecurity and hunger. Samuel, a 22-year-old African-American junior, explained: *I want to graduate in time because I want to be a teacher. I want that to be my future, and I want my future to come as quickly as possible. I don't want to take a break just to get food money. I want to be able to do both. I know I can do both.* Erika shared her story:

I have really high expectations of myself and hold myself to a really high standard. That didn't change. There is very little that would get me to leave. I eventually want to get my doctorate and teach. For a while I wanted to work for the United Nations with refugees. I have really high goals, and I'm going to do all I can to get to them. I won't let dropping out be an option for myself, but I feel like a lot of people in my situation, that would have been an option for them. I have never let myself make that an option.

Brianna is a 23-year-old African-American senior who is married. She explained: *Knowing my goals. I'm not always going to be this poor. Knowing that one day I will be in a position where I wouldn't even think about food. And knowing that it's up to me to keep the ball rolling no matter how hard it gets. Now that's one thing that I get that's good from my family...that resilience.* Destiny, a 21-year-old African-American junior, added: *I know I need to get a degree. It's what I need to do. It's like my proof to the world that, hey, I'm disciplined. That's really good. I'm a disciplined individual and that I need to get a degree. But also, I just want to be done, so my motivation is to finish, so I can be done as quickly as possible.*

Participants reported that family expectations also motivated them to remain in college (14%). Students said that they did not want to let their parents down or that they have promised their parents that they would attend college. Julie, an 18-year-old White freshman, noted: *I kind of feel like I have to. I gotta get that degree (laughs). I've got to make sure my parents don't hate me. It's like, if I dropped out of school, they would probably get mad.* Trinity, a 20-year-old African-American junior, explained: *I would say it's my parents because in my family we don't believe in dropping out. There's no point in dropping out because you didn't drop out throughout elementary school or high school, so why would you in college? Why would you drop out now from university? Like, you came so far just to drop out, you know? And I don't want to work at a fast food restaurant the rest of my life.* Orisa is a 21-year-old African-American junior whose family is from Nigeria. She stated: *I don't want to put my kids through that. I also don't want to put my family through that. I told both my parents that when I get successful, I'm going to build them this big mansion. And, like I said, we were from Nigeria, and so any time I feel like giving up, I always remember how hard my parents worked to bring us from there to here, and so I'm not going to disappoint them.*

Other participants said they were motivated by the example that they were setting for their children or younger siblings. Brittany is an 18-year-old African-American/White freshman who lived in the dorms. She explained:

> *It's actually my family. I think for me because I'm the oldest out of my sisters, I want to show them that just because we are from a poor family or we don't have a certain amount of money for something, that doesn't mean we can't go to school. That doesn't mean we can't do better for ourselves. So, it's really my sisters that motivate me every day to get out of bed and go to class, because I want them to know they have a lot of options in life.*

Lastly, nine percent of participants noted that food insecurity is a temporary problem and that school is more important than hunger. Naomi, a 21-year-old African-American senior, stated: *I feel like food insecurity is a temporary problem that I've found ways to overcome. I feel school (and this is kind of funny) is more important. I'm here. I've been doing this. This is what I want to do with my life, and I'm not going to let me not eating get in the way of that. I'm going to finish what I started, regardless if I have food to eat or not.* Kevin, a 23-year-old African-American junior, said: *I mean, I could quit school and work full time and do well on my own. But I wouldn't be happy with my quality of life. So, I want to get a degree and then go to grad school. And I know that I'm gonna have to face these struggles, you know? Get through it, but just knowing that it's temporary helps.*

Food insecure college students have additional hurdles to overcome toward academic success. Hadley and Crooks (2012) note that food insecure households make trade-offs with competing demands of resources. For college students, these trade-offs are the competing demands between academic success, diet and health, and having enough resources for their livelihood. Research shows that poor academic achievement is linked to poor diet, fatigue, difficulties concentrating, poor mental health, and reduced cognitive function. Food insecure college students are more likely to be working, have less access to academic resources (such as textbooks), are more stressed, and think about food when they should be focused on schoolwork. Patton-López et al. (2014) note, "food insecurity, as a potential consequence of the increasing cost of higher education, and its likely impact on student health, learning, and social outcomes, should not be considered an accepted aspect of the impoverished student experience, but a major student health priority" (209).

REFERENCES

Alaimo, Katherine, Christine M. Olson, and Edward A. Frongillo Jr. 2001. Food Insufficiency and American School-Aged Children's Cognitive, Academic, and Psychosocial Development. *Pediatrics* 108 (1): 44–53.

Allen, Alejandro C. 2019. *Study Hard, Eat Less: Exploring Food Insecurity Among College Students.* Master's Thesis, Texas State University, San Marcos, TX.

Allen, Cara Cliburn, and Nathan F. Alleman. 2019. A Private Struggle at a Private Institution: Effects of Student Hunger on Social and Academic Experiences. *Journal of College Student Development* 60 (1): 52–69. https://doi.org/10.1353/csd.2019.0003.

Camelo, Karen, and Marta Elliott. 2019. Food Insecurity and Academic Achievement Among College Students at a Public University in the United States. *Journal of College Student Development* 60 (3): 307–318. https://doi.org/10.1353/csd.2019.0028.

Carnevale, Anthony, Stephen Rose, and Ban Cheah. 2014. *The College Payoff: Education, Occupations, Lifetime Earnings*. Center on Education and the Workforce. https://1gyhoq479ufd3yna29x7ubjn-wpengine.netdna-ssl.com/wp-content/uploads/collegepayoff-completed.pdf. Accessed 10 April 2019.

Cole, Stephen, and Elinor G. Barber. 2003. *Increasing Faculty Diversity: The Occupational Choices of High-Achieving Minority Students*. Cambridge, MA: Harvard University Press.

Eisenberg, Daniel, Sara Goldrick-Rab, Sarah Ketchen Lipson, and Katharine Broton. 2016. *Too Distressed to Learn? Mental Health among Community College Students*. Report, March. https://hope4college.com/wp-content/uploads/2018/09/Wisconsin_HOPE_Lab-Too_Distressed_To_Learn.pdf. Accessed 12 May 2019.

El Zein, Aseel, Karla Shelnutt, Sarah Colby, Melissa Olfert, Kendra Kattelmann, Onikia Brown, Tandalayo Kidd, et al. 2017. The Prevalence of Food Insecurity and Its Association with Health and Academic Outcomes Among College Freshmen. *Advances in Nutrition* 8 (1): 4. https://doi.org/10.1093/advances/8.1.4.

El Zein, Aseel, Karla P. Shelnutt, Sarah Colby, Melissa J. Vilaro, Wenjun Zhou, Geoffrey Greene, Melissa D. Olfert, Kristin Riggsbee, Jesse Stabile Morrell, and Anne E. Mathews. 2019. Prevalence and Correlates of Food Insecurity Among U.S. College Students: A Multi-institutional Study. *BMC Public Health* 19 (1). https://doi.org/10.1186/s12889-019-6943-6.

Farahbakhsh, Jasmine, Mahitab Hanbazaza, Geoff D.C. Ball, Anna P. Farmer, Katerina Maximova, and Noreen D. Willows. 2017. Food Insecure Student Clients of a University-based Food Bank Have Compromised Health, Dietary Intake and Academic Quality. *Nutrition & Dietetics* 74 (1): 67–73. https://doi.org/10.1111/1747-0080.12307.

Goldrick-Rab, Sara. 2016. *Paying the Price: College Costs, Financial Aid, and the Betrayal of the American Dream*. Chicago, IL: University of Chicago Press.

Goldrick-Rab, Sara, Christine Baker-Smith, Vanessa Coca, Elizabeth Looker, and Tiffani Williams. 2019. *College and University Basic Needs Insecurity: A National #RealCollege Survey Report*. Report, April. https://hope4college.com/wp-content/uploads/2019/04/HOPE_realcollege_National_report_digital.pdf. Accessed 18 May 2019.

Hadley, Craig, and Deborah L. Crooks. 2012. Coping and the Biosocial Consequences of Food Insecurity in the 21st Century. *American Journal of Physical Anthropology* 149 (S55): 72–94. https://doi.org/10.1002/ajpa.22161.

Hagedorn, Rebecca L., and Melissa D. Olfert. 2018. Food Insecurity and Behavioral Characteristics for Academic Success in Young Adults Attending an Appalachian University. *Nutrients* 10 (3): 361. https://doi.org/10.3390/nu10030361.

Hinton, Ivora, Jessica Howell, Elizabeth Merwin, Steven N. Stern, Sarah Turner, Ishan Williams, and Melvin Wilson. 2010. The Educational Pipeline for Health Care Professionals. *Journal of Human Resources* 45 (1): 116–156. https://doi.org/10.3368/jhr.45.1.116.

Hout, Michael. 2012. Social and Economic Returns to College Education in the United States. *Annual Review of Sociology* 38 (1): 379–400. https://doi.org/10.1146/annurev.soc.012809.102503.

Hughes, Roger, Irene Serebryanikova, Katherine Donaldson, and Michael Leveritt. 2011. Student Food Insecurity: The Skeleton in the University Closet. *Nutrition & Dietetics* 68 (1): 27–32. https://doi.org/10.1111/j.1747-0080.2010.01496.x.

Jyoti, Diana F., Edward A. Frongillo, and Sonya J. Jones. 2005. Food Insecurity Affects School Childrens Academic Performance, Weight Gain, and Social Skills. *The Journal of Nutrition* 135 (12): 2831–2839. https://doi.org/10.1093/jn/135.12.2831.

Kleinman, Ronald E., J. Michael Murphy, Michelle Little, Maria Pagano, Cheryl A. Wehler, Kenneth Regal, and Michael S. Jellinek. 1998. Hunger in Children in the United States: Potential Behavioral and Emotional Correlates. *Pediatrics* 101 (1): E3. https://doi.org/10.1542/peds.101.1.e3.

Ma, Jennifer, Matea Pender, and Meredith Welch. 2016. *Education Pay 2016: The Benefits of Higher Education for Individuals and Society*. Report. New York: College Board. https://trends.collegeboard.org/sites/default/files/education-pays-2016-full-report.pdf. Accessed 15 Apr 2019.

Maroto, Maya E., Anastasia Snelling, and Henry Linck. 2015. Food Insecurity among Community College Students: Prevalence and Association with Grade Point Average. *Community College Journal of Research and Practice* 39 (6): 515–526. https://doi.org/10.1080/10668926.2013.850758.

Martinez, Suzanna M., Katie Maynard, and Lorrene D. Ritchie. 2016. *Student Food Access and Security Study. Global Food Initiative*. Report. Division of Agriculture and Natural Resources, University of California. https://regents.universityofcalifornia.edu/regmeet/july16/e1attach.pdf.   Accessed 3 May 2018.

Martinez, Suzanna M., Edward A. Frongillo, Cindy Leung, and Lorrene Ritchie. 2018. No Food for Thought: Food Insecurity Is Related to Poor Mental Health and Lower Academic Performance Among Students in California's Public University System. *Journal of Health Psychology*: 135910531878302, June 1. https://doi.org/10.1177/1359105318783028.

McArthur, Laura Helena, Lanae Ball, Ariel C. Danek, and Donald Holbert. 2018. A High Prevalence of Food Insecurity Among University Students in Appalachia Reflects a Need for Educational Interventions and Policy Advocacy. *Journal of Nutrition Education and Behavior* 50 (6): 564–572. https://doi.org/10.1016/j.jneb.2017.10.011.

Meza, Anthony, Emily Altman, Suzanna Martinez, and Cindy W. Leung. 2018. "It's a Feeling That One Is Not Worth Food": A Qualitative Study Exploring the Psychosocial Experience and Academic Consequences of Food Insecurity Among College Students. *Journal of the Academy of Nutrition and Dietetics*, December 12. https://doi.org/10.1016/j.jand.2018.09.006.

Morris, Loran, Sylvia Smith, Jeremy Davis, and Dawn Bloyd Null. 2016. The Prevalence of Food Security and Insecurity Among Illinois University Students Response Letter. *Journal of Nutrition Education and Behavior* 48 (9): 376–382. https://doi.org/10.1016/j.jneb.2016.07.017.

Murphy, J. Michael, Cheryl A. Wehler, Maria E. Pagano, Michelle Little, Ronald E. Kleinman, and Michael S. Jellinek. 1998. Relationship Between Hunger and Psychosocial Functioning in Low-Income American Children. *Journal of the American Academy of Child & Adolescent Psychiatry* 37 (2): 163–170. https://doi.org/10.1097/00004583-199802000-00008.

O'Neill, Marissa, and Jennifer Maguire. 2017. College Students Self-Reported Food Insecurity and Correlations with Health and Academic Performance. *Journal of Behavioral & Social Sciences* 4: 34–40.

Patton-López, Megan M., Daniel F. López-Cevallos, Doris I. Cancel-Tirado, and Leticia Vazquez. 2014. Prevalence and Correlates of Food Insecurity among Students Attending a Midsize Rural University in Oregon. *Journal of Nutrition Education and Behavior* 46 (3): 209–214. https://doi.org/10.1016/j.jneb.2013.10.007.

Payne-Sturges, Devon C., Allison Tjaden, Kimberly M. Caldeira, Kathryn B. Vincent, and Amelia M. Arria. 2018. Student Hunger on Campus: Food Insecurity Among College Students and Implications for Academic Institutions. *American Journal of Health Promotion* 32 (2): 349–354. https://doi.org/10.1177/0890117117719620.

Phillips, Erica, Anne McDaniel, and Alicia Croft. 2018. Food Insecurity and Academic Disruption Among College Students. *Journal of Student Affairs Research and Practice* 55 (4): 353–372. https://doi.org/10.1080/19496591.2018.1470003.

Reid, Lori L. 2000. *The Consequences of Food Insecurity for Child Well-Being: An Analysis of Children's School Achievement, Psychological Well-Being, and Health.* Report. Department of Sociology, Florida State University. Joint Center for Poverty Research. http://citeseerx.ist.psu.edu/viewdoc/download?doi=10.1.1.194.7912&rep=rep1&type=pdf.

Shankar, Priya, Rainjade Chung, and Deborah A. Frank. 2017. Association of Food Insecurity with Children's Behavioral, Emotional, and Academic Outcomes: A Systematic Review. *Journal of Developmental and Behavioral Pediatrics* 38 (2): 135–150. https://doi.org/10.1097/DBP.0000000000000383.

Silva, Meghan R., Whitney L. Kleinert, A. Victoria Sheppard, Kathryn A. Cantrell, Darren J. Freeman-Coppadge, Elena Tsoy, Tangela Roberts, and Melissa Pearrow. 2015. The Relationship Between Food Security, Housing Stability, and School Performance Among College Students in an Urban University. *Journal of College Student Retention: Research, Theory & Practice* 19 (3): 284–299. https://doi.org/10.1177/1521025115621918.

Simon, Ashley Uyeshiro, Stephanie Bianco, Keiko Goto, and Jenny Breed. 2018. Factors Associated with Food Insecurity and Food Assistance Program Participation Among University Students. *Californian Journal of Health Promotion* 16 (1): 73–78.

van Woerden, Irene, Daniel Hruschka, and Meg Bruening. 2018. Food Insecurity Negatively Impacts Academic Performance. *Journal of Public Affairs*: E1864, November 26. https://doi.org/10.1002/pa.1864.

Watson, Tyler D., Hannah Malan, Deborah Glik, and Suzanna M. Martinez. 2017. College Students Identify University Support for Basic Needs and Life Skills as Key Ingredient in Addressing Food Insecurity on Campus. *California Agriculture* 71 (3): 130–138. https://doi.org/10.3733/ca.2017a0023.

Weaver, Robert R., Nicole A. Vaugh, Sean P. Hendricks, Penny E. McPherson-Myers, Qian Jia, Shari L. Willis, and Kevin P. Rescigo. 2019. University Student Food Insecurity and Academic Performance. *Journal of American College Health*, May 7. https://doi.org/10.1080/07448481.2019.1600522.

Wooten, Ruth, Marsha Spence, Sarah Colby, and Elizabeth Anderson Steeves. 2018. Assessing Food Insecurity Prevalence and Associated Factors among College Students Enrolled in a University in the Southeast USA. *Public Health Nutrition* 22 (3): 383–390. https://doi.org/10.1017/s1368980018003531.

CHAPTER 6

Solutions

Abstract This chapter begins with a discussion on the importance of evaluating programs designed to reduce food insecurity in order to understand and measure their success. Next, I discuss the rise in food pantries across the nation, followed by a discussion of the evaluation of the UNT Food Pantry. Pantry clients were asked to evaluate, on a scale of 1–10 (10 being the highest), several aspects of their experience, including topics related to overall experience, confidentiality, helpfulness of the pantry, opinions about the amount of food, how the pantry helped, panty items most wanted, and opinions about the layout of the pantry and the hours. Next, I discuss other local solutions suggested by UNT Food Pantry clients. Finally, I briefly discuss various programs that are occurring across the nation, including a discussion of current legislation designed to bolster attention to food security among college students.

Keywords Food insecurity • Evaluation • Solutions • Legislation

In a new edited volume, *Food Insecurity on Campus: Action and Intervention*, Katharine Broton and Clare L. Cady (2020) provide an overview of many strategies across the nation to combat food insecurity among college students. They emphasize that solving the food insecurity crisis on college campuses does not have one solution. Food pantries fill a particular niche of a short-term food solution to students who have the resources to carry, store, and prepare the food. Meal vouchers at university cafeterias might serve better for students who are on campus and have no kitchen to prepare food. Increased SNAP benefits might provide additional long-term relieve to financial stress. Broton and Cady encourage a multifaceted holistic approach to reduce campus food insecurity rather than a single solution. They suggest that universities should collect data (including student voices) to understand the local context of their specific university—student issues, resources, stakeholders, champions—and tailor programs that will optimize positive outcomes for students (see Broton and Cady 2020). I wholeheartedly support this model because understanding the meaning of particular beliefs, experiences, and behaviors within the local context is one of the hallmarks of ethnography and cultural anthropology—my own academic discipline and the foundation of this research.

An important key aspect to food insecurity solutions is evaluation of those solutions. Universities need to collect data on the local context and what solutions might work given their campus parameters and priorities, but it is equally important to collect evaluative data to understand *if* those programs are working. There has been very little work in the area of food insecurity program evaluation (Goldrick-Rab et al. 2018a). Sara Goldrick-Rab and the Hope Center for College, Community, and Justice are trying to change this by developing a body of high-quality evidence on effective practices that can be used by other universities that hope to implement similar programs. Goldrick-Rab et al. (2018c) support the use of experimental outcome evaluations. In order to assess if the program is reaching its desired outcomes (improved academic success), this type of evaluation uses randomized controlled trials to follow two groups. One group consists of randomly selected qualified students who participate in the program. The second group consists of randomly selected students, similar in characteristics to the first group, who serve as the comparison group. The comparison group is studied but does not receive program benefits during the research project.

Goldrick-Rab and colleagues have established two experimental outcome evaluations of food insecurity solutions. The first evaluation is of a meal voucher program at Bunker Hill Community College in Boston. Katharine M. Broton and Sara Goldrick-Rab are tracking the outcomes of students in the program and a select group of students not in the program. Specifically, they are assessing "students' educational performance including course completion rates, GPA, persistence and credential attainment, and surveying students to learn about their well-being, including levels of food insecurity and stress" (Goldrick-Rab et al. 2018a, 6). The second evaluation is of a food scholarship program at Houston Community College. Daphne Hernandez and Sara Goldrick-Rab are tracking the amount of food, types of food, and the educational outcomes of 350 recipients of food scholarships, as well as a comparison group of similar students not in the program (Goldrick-Rab et al. 2018a). Evaluation data from initiatives such as these are vital, particularly for administrators and policymakers who value evidence-based data to understand which of these programs are producing positive outcomes.

At the time of the UNT research study, the UNT Food Pantry was the only formal food-related resource available to UNT students.[1] Therefore, I begin this chapter discussing the rise in food pantries across the nation. Next, I discuss the evaluation of the UNT Food Pantry by panty clients, including topics related to overall experience, confidentiality, helpfulness of the pantry, opinions about the amount of food, how the pantry helped, panty items most wanted, and opinions about the layout of the pantry and pantry hours. Next, I discuss other local solutions suggested by UNT Food Pantry clients. Finally, I briefly discuss various programs that are occurring across the nation, including a discussion of current legislation designed to bolster attention to food insecurity among college students.

6.1   COLLEGE AND UNIVERSITY FOOD PANTRIES

One major indication that colleges and universities across the country are taking notice of student food insecurity is the rapid growth in food pantries on college campuses. The College and University Food Bank Alliance (CUFBA) was co-founded in 2012 by the Michigan State Student Food Bank and the Oregon State University Food Pantry with a membership of 15 schools. As of 2019, the membership is over 700 member schools. The mission of the alliance is to offer support, training, and resources to campuses that offer food insecurity initiatives that serve students (Goldrick-Rab et al. 2018a). CUFBA partnered with The Hope Center for College, Community, and Justice to conduct the first-ever national survey of campus food pantries. The importance of this survey work is to explore how campus food pantries are implemented, managed, and resourced across the nation in order to collect data on their efficacy. This data will provide insight into what works, what does not work, and what needs improvement (see Goldrick-Rab et al. 2018a for the full report).

6.1.1   UNT Food Pantry Evaluation

As noted, the UNT Food Pantry launched its opening in January 2015, just a few months after the pilot study of food insecurity at UNT. In this current study, which started in February 2017, the Dean of Students and I decided it was time to evaluate the UNT Food Pantry since it had been serving UNT students for two years. However, I did not conduct an outcome evaluation that would test improved academic success of students. Rather, I conducted a process evaluation that focused on understanding how the pantry was doing, the capacity of staff and resources to serve the needs of the clients, and what was working and not working (see Butler 2015). I used a mixed-method research design to capture a quantitative assessment of average opinions, as well as a qualitative inquiry to allow pantry clients to explain their sentiment, experiences, and authentic insights for each topic. An evaluation report was provided to the UNT Dean of Students in December 2017. They have been using the data to discuss and implement programmatic changes and improvements, which will be discussed in Chap. 7. I report mean scores on a scale of 1 to 10 (with 10 being the best) for each topic evaluated. A deeper analysis was conducted to identify any major mean score differences within potential independent variables (i.e. age, gender, ethnicity, year in college, marital status, living arrangements, federal food insecurity group, childhood food insecurity, etc.). Any statistically significant findings will be discussed below. It can be assumed that if deeper analysis is not discussed, no significant findings were discovered.

6.1.1.1 Overall Pantry Experience

Participants were asked to score their overall experience using the UNT Food Pantry and gave a mean score of 8.17. Interestingly, participants' reasons for a specific overall experience score were similar no matter if the participant rated the experience a four or an eight. Participants were overwhelmingly appreciative of their experiences with the pantry. Many mentioned how friendly and accommodating the staff at the Dean of Students department was, and how they felt that the pantry was a good resource. Many mentioned that they expected to feel stigma or judgment before going to the pantry for the first time; however, those feelings never materialized because of the staff's respectful treatment of them during the visit. There was also a general appreciation for the free bag to carry their groceries (Fig. 6.1).

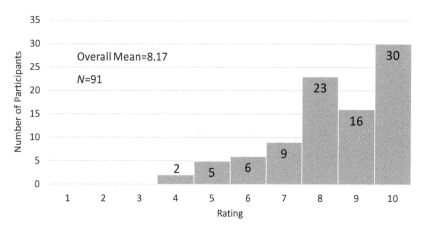

Fig. 6.1 Overall pantry experience

Participants gave very little criticism about their overall experience at the food pantry. However, for those who did express critical judgment, a few patterns emerged. Most commonly, participants cited the need for variety as their main reason for any critical judgment of their overall experience at the pantry. In stating the need for variety, many students explained that they understood why the donations were not more varied, but that they still wanted variety in their diets. Ashley, a 19-year-old White junior who lived on campus, said: *It's silly to look a gift horse in the mouth, but it could use a little more variety. Maybe that's just the mindset of the people who are donating. They're like, 'oh, yea, they need vegetables and soup.' I don't know. I guess it was just all the same stuff. It was just one rack of the same pretty much.* Participants also talked about the quality and nutritious value of the food. Makayla, a 20-year-old African-American junior, stated that in her nutrition class, she learned that foods high in preservatives actually hurt a person's digestive tract. She pointed out that shelved foods, such as those in the pantry, are preserved in this manner and she questioned their nutritional value. James, a 20-year-old African-American sophomore, stated *I'm looking for high quality, delicious foods* and *I don't like peas at all like. I hate peas, and there's so many cans of peas in there. I'm not trying to be picky, but I want healthy food that is also delicious and it's not peas.* Another student stated that she could use the canned foods available, but items with a higher nutritional value, like bread, milk, dairy, and meats, were more important to her.

The next most mentioned criticism was a dislike of being escorted from the Dean of Students department on the fourth floor to the food pantry on the third floor by a member of the Dean of Students staff (see Chap. 7 for post-study modifications). Other comments included a need for more instruction before being left to get their items in the pantry and a need for better labeling within the pantry.

6.1.1.2 Confidentiality

Confidentiality was rated with a slightly higher mean score (8.29) than overall experience. During the interviews, many participants stated fear of judgment and stigma from their peers and the university as an original obstacle they faced before their first visit to the pantry. Many of the same clients expressed relief from these fears and attributed that relief to the confidentiality offered to them by the pantry sign-in process and the lack of judgment they felt from the staff (Fig. 6.2).

One of the main items mentioned as an assurance of confidentiality was that the students did not need to provide their names or any information other than their student ID number upon signing in to the pantry. Many also said that they were reassured that the visit would be kept confidential, and they had never been given reason to think that their privacy had in any way been violated.

Critique of the food pantry's confidentiality mainly centered around the need to go to the Dean of Students department to sign in. Many

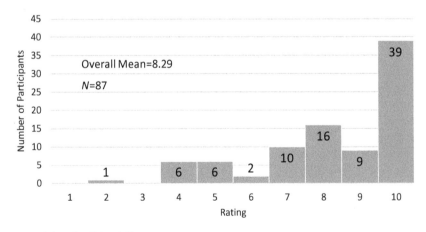

Fig. 6.2   Confidentiality

participants stated that they knew a lot of people in that area of the University Union because the student organizations' offices are located near the Dean of Students. A few clients suggested that a sign-in sheet placed so the student could request a pantry visit non-verbally would increase confidentiality while in the Dean of Students department. One student mistakenly thought that the free bag given to students for food was labeled with "UNT Food Pantry." This student thought that their trip to the food pantry was not as confidential as they wanted because they were seen walking across campus with a food pantry bag. Actually, the bag was labeled with "Dean of Students," but this misperception ties back to discussions about stigma, embarrassment, and discretion.

6.1.1.3 Helpfulness of Pantry

Participants were asked to rate how much the food pantry helped them in the moment that they needed it. The majority gave the food pantry a perfect score of ten for helpfulness, with a mean score of 8.99. The main reason given was that they really needed food and the food pantry provided that food. Jana, a 22-year-old White senior, noted: *It's helped a lot. For instance, I would have no food and then just being able to go and just come home with a bag full of groceries was really helpful. It helped me academically, because I'd be able to go to class on a full stomach.* Erika, a 19-year-old White sophomore who lived on campus, also commented how the food pantry helped with her studies: *I know that I had two tests that week, and I was able to study and do decently well on them. I was able to feel a lot better for a few weeks while I had the food, and I was happier because I knew it was there. I didn't feel like I was gonna have to figure out where it was coming from.* Many students said that even if the pantry did not provide them with all that they needed, being able to supplement their groceries with food from the pantry made it so that they would make it to their next paycheck without skipping too many meals. Molly is a 19-year-old White freshman who lived on campus with a meal plan that did not include weekend meals. She stated that the food pantry *helped stretch out the money, or my meal plan FLEX dollars, a little bit longer.* Others stated that the pantry was quick, efficient, and provided a judgment-free resource in addition to helping them with their immediate needs of sustenance. A few students tied the helpfulness of the pantry into their academic success: *I feel good. I can focus on my books* (Fig. 6.3).

Participants who were more critical of the help they received from the pantry were unhappy with the variety and the quality of the food. Some

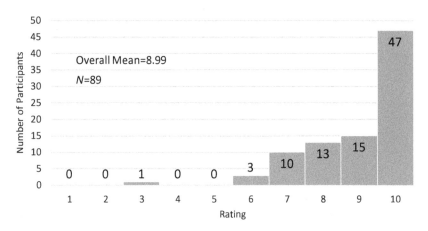

Fig. 6.3 Helpfulness of pantry

students stated that they used the pantry food as sides to meals, while others stated that they would prefer complete meals. A few students stated that they were not aware of the food pantry when they really needed it and only found out about the resource once they had already gotten through the worst of their hunger.

Deeper analysis showed two significant differences in mean scores for helpfulness. Female participants had a mean score of 9.19, whereas male participants had a mean score of 8.63. This difference was statistically significant; $t(85) = -1.856$, $p < .05$. Participants who experienced childhood food insecurity had a mean helpfulness score of 9.21, whereas those who did not experience childhood food insecurity had a mean score of 8.63. This difference was statistically significant; $t(87) = 1.856$, $p < .05$. No clear sub-themes emerged to explain these differences, so additional research is needed to fully understand these differences. One 22-year-old African-American female student who rated the helpfulness of the pantry a ten talked about her appreciation of non-food items: *It helped a lot because the very first time I was out of toothpaste and other stuff and I went and got all of that. So, it was like everything that I was needing, I knew that they had. So that really helped me a lot and saved money that I didn't even have. Those items are just as important as food in today's world. We all need deodorant. We all need toothpaste. Women need tampons. And so, it helps.* A few participants who did not experience food insecurity as children and rated the helpfulness low made comments like *I wanted things that weren't there* and *they didn't always have what I was looking for*. Possibly those without previous food insecurity experience had higher expectations of what the pantry could offer.

6.1.1.4 Adequacy of the Amount of Food

The last-scaled question asked participants to rate the adequacy of the amount of food they received from the UNT Food Pantry. The mean score was 8.41. Participants who gave scores of ten praised the fact that they could take as much food as they wanted as long as it fits into the given bag, and that they were not monitored while taking food. Tonya, a 23-year-old African-American senior, shared: *Because whenever you go, they make it known that you can take whatever you need. And nobody's in the room with you, so it just takes off the pressure of feeling like ... okay, well, let me just get this or let me just get that. They close the door, and they're just like, all right, you know, have at it. So, then you're able to go through and get the things that you need to get without the pressure.* Many participants also added that they knew they could go back to the food pantry for more food if they needed it. Participants again noted that the pantry served its purpose in helping them through their period of hunger and food insecurity (Fig. 6.4).

Students who gave low scores for satisfaction with the amount of food stated that the food was not enough. They commented that the food was snack food, side items, or that the selection lacked variety. Some students

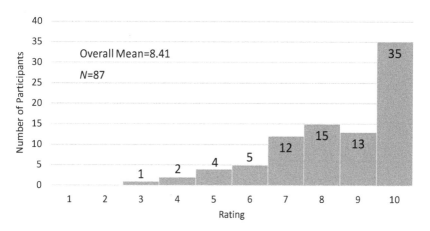

Fig. 6.4 Adequacy of the amount of food

stated that they had allergies which further limited their available choices, both from the food pantry and the cafeterias.

Deeper analysis showed a significant difference in the mean scores of participants when they were separated by U.S. Food Security Categories. A one-way between-groups ANOVA was performed. The assumption of homogeneity of variances was tested and satisfied based on Levene's F Test, $F(4,82) = .92$, $p = .456$. The independent between-groups ANOVA yielded a statistically significant effect, $F(4,82) = 3.019$, $p = .022$. A post-hoc Tukey test showed that marginally food secure students (mean = 6.5) and low food secure students (mean = 8.8) differ significantly in their mean scores ($p < .05$). Out of the 87 participants who rated satisfaction with the amount of food received, only 8 (9%) were marginally food secure and 15 (17%) were low food secure. Though these percentages are fairly low, their mean scores were significantly different so it is beneficial to identify characteristics that might contribute to these differences. Marginal food secure participants, who were the least satisfied with the amount of food at the pantry, included the largest concentration of married students (40% of all married students) and graduate students (50% of all graduate students) and had a large number of international students (25% of all international students). All of them lived in apartments, 88 percent had no experience with childhood food insecurity, and 75 percent had access to nutritious foods while food insecure. Their ethnicity varied, as did their age groups though the majority were 23–29 years old. By comparison, the key characteristics that stand out among low food secure participants, who were the most satisfied with the amount of food at the pantry, are age (81% 18–22 years old) and ethnicity (56% African-American).

Participants were asked more specific questions about the adequacy of the amount of food they received. How long it lasted? Was it intended for a short time? A specific hurdle? The largest response from participants (43%) was that they got enough food to last them for about two weeks. Many stated that the food was used to supplement their groceries or other foods. Sixteen percent of participants stated that they needed the food to last them through the weekend. These students lived on campus and had meal plans during the week, but over the weekend their meal plans were not available. Students without transportation stated that they could only find rides to and from the grocery store every few weeks or once a month, and they needed the food pantry items to last until their next ride was available.

6.1.1.5 Pantry Items Most Wanted

When participants were asked what other items they would like to see available in the UNT Food Pantry, many stated that they were aware of the limitations of shelved foods (the pantry did not have cold storage at the time of data collection). Answers were given based on what students would like to see if the food pantry were to have the resources necessary to store any type of food item. Table 6.1 lists the items in order by the

Table 6.1 Pantry items most wanted by clients (items listed by frequency of request)

Staples	Snacks	Food for meals	Non-food items	Other
Vegetables	Granola bars	Pasta	Feminine products	Frozen foods
Fruit	Popcorn	Cereal	Toiletries	Refrigerated food
Bread	Chips	Rice	Deodorant	Juices
Milk	Crackers	Canned soup	Can opener	Water
Lactose free milk	Fruit cups	Beans	Toothbrush	Coffee
Peanut butter	Protein bars	Oatmeal	Soap	Cooking oil
Meat	Pop-tarts	Canned/boxed meal	Toilet paper	Spices
Eggs	Fruit snacks	Pizza	Toothpaste	Low sodium foods
Butter	Dried fruit	Canned chicken	Clothing	Baby formula
Cheese	Pringles	Macaroni & cheese	Utensils	Soy foods
Sugar	Twinkies	Rice-a-Roni	Umbrellas	Vitamins
Tortillas	Snack cakes	SpaghettiOs's	Hair products for people of color	Infant goods
Flour	Trail mix	Vienna sausages	Floss	Portable containers
Jelly	Almonds	Chili	Wipes	Fresh foods
	Pudding	Pasta sauce	Napkins	Healthier foods
	Nutella	Instant potatoes	Pregnancy tests	Crystal light
	Candy	Hamburger helper	Trash bags	Mayonnaise
	Canned cheese	Quinoa	Bowls	Tea
		Breakfast items	Shampoo	Tofu
		Ravioli	Straws	Almond milk
		Canned tuna	Razors	Ketchup
		Broths	Mouthwash	Pet food
		Couscous	Tylenol	
		Lunchables		
		Spam		
		Vegetarian chili		

Table 6.2   Sub-categories of pantry items most wanted by clients

Vegetables	Fruits	Frozen foods	Meat
Carrots	Fruit cups	Pizza	Chicken
Potatoes	Tomato	Ice cream	Chili
Green beans	Apples	Vegetable stir fry	Hot dog
Lettuce	Oranges	Eggo waffles	Sausage
Spinach	Canned peaches	Taquitos	Sandwich meat
Dark leafy greens		Frozen dinners	
Chickpeas		Hot pockets	

number of times each item was requested in interviews. Some food categories (such as vegetables or frozen foods) have specific lists of requested foods and are listed in Table 6.2.

In addition to specific items wanted, many students stated that they wanted variety or different options and some reliability in selection. In other words, they would like to know what to expect to see available when they go. Some students stated that having menu ideas or different options for what foods to take from the pantry in order to eat a balanced meal would help them almost as much as the food itself. Instant versions of items (such as rice or potatoes) were requested as often as traditional versions. An idea given to counteract a lack of variety was to have gift cards available for groceries at times when the food pantry was out of staple items.

6.1.1.6 Layout and Pantry Hours

When asked about the layout of the pantry, 40 percent of the students said the pantry was fine as is and well organized. There were, however, slightly more students (43%) who felt that the pantry was small. Descriptors such as "claustrophobic," "cramped," and "it felt like an afterthought" were used to portray how the small room made them feel. Besides the size of the pantry, there was little to say about pantry layout. A handful of students would have liked to see more instructions posted on the walls about what they could take and how they should choose their foods. In other parts of the interview, many students expressed a want for nutritional guidance, instruction in meal planning, and guidance for how best to select foods from the food pantry. Posting signs for this purpose may be an avenue of support for these materials.

Participants were asked about their opinion of the pantry's hours, and 64 percent said the hours were adequate to fit their needs. Requests for changes to hours included keeping the pantry open until 8:00 pm every night and opening for some limited hours on the weekends.

6.2   STUDENT-SUGGESTED UNT SOLUTIONS

Formal programs to alleviate campus food insecurity are being implemented across the country and will be discussed in the next section. The goal of this section is to understand what solutions UNT food insecure students think would work in the local context of their university. Some of these solutions may overlap with existing programs elsewhere, but rather than branching out into that national discussion here, this section will focus on UNT student suggestions for UNT students.

Participants were asked a series of questions about other ways UNT could help students who struggle to find food or worry about food, what type of solutions would help them most personally, and what types of programs they would not use if offered by UNT. Most participants struggled to think of additional solutions and suggested improvements to the resources that were already present on campus. Some participants spoke about how difficult it must be to offer solutions while also considering the stigma which may cause students to avoid those solutions.

6.2.1   Broadcast Resources

More than half of the participants (51%) suggested the need to increase the broadcasting of resources that are available. Many participants observed that other topics dealing with sensitive issues (take back the night, mental health help, etc.) were broadcasted campus-wide, but they felt that hunger and food insecurity did not receive the same level of broadcasting. As discussed in Chap. 3, students wanted to increase the conversation at UNT about issues related to food insecurity. They wanted more information about the resources that were available to all students. Participants acknowledged the paradox in wanting more e-mails from the university since they often did not read their university e-mails. However, they said that they need multiple, repeated messaging in order for the information to sink in.

The participants listed many different methods for broadcasting resources (see Table 6.3). Several of the methods would only happen once

Table 6.3 Avenues to broadcast resources

Avenues to broadcast resources (ordered by frequency mentioned)
• Twitter
• Email
• Online courses announcements
• Orientation
• Announcements in class by instructor
• Print flyers/yard sign throughout campus
• Department announcements
• Tabling event with free food/snacks
• Include on the syllabus

per semester (at orientation or putting information in the syllabus), while others (Twitter, email, etc.) could be utilized much more frequently. A standard procedure of advertising the presence of campus hunger resources (and resources around Denton) would establish dependable channels which students could rely on for information about food resources. Developing a checklist of standard channels to broadcast hunger resources could help to implement standardized dispersal of information about those resources. Twitter was the most mentioned method to broadcast resources. On the other hand, interestingly, one student stated that if more people knew about the pantry, she would most likely stop using it due to fear of running into other students who she knows. This sentiment reinforces the need for discussing a broader, a campus-wide conversation about stigma, shame, and discretion.

6.2.2   Free Food Events

The next most consistent suggestion for combating hunger at UNT was to have more free food events. Twenty-five percent of the students interviewed mentioned this as a direct action to combat hunger. Participants referenced free food events, such as Earth Day, where they were happily surprised with the presence of free food. A deeper analysis highlights that some students who fall into the very low food secure category on the U.S. Food Security Survey considered themselves as food secure due to their utilization of free food events that were regularly offered on campus or near campus.

In suggesting free food events, participants pointed out that these events help all the students at the university, not just food insecure students. Destiny, a 21-year-old African-American junior, suggested:

I think some things that might help is when they have events on campus, have a quick meal available. I think that would be great. A lot of times you do see them doing that, especially if they're out on the library mall. They have little food snacks that you can pick up really quick and stuff like that. I think that's really great. Because there are a lot of people I know who are commuters, and so when they see stuff on campus where you can get free food, they're like, 'I for sure will do that.' And so, I think that's really, really helpful. Even if it's a small little snack, I think it does make a difference, especially if you're on the go between classes and stuff. So, I think that would help.

6.2.3   Multiple Other Suggestions

There were several suggestions which were mentioned consistently but by fewer students. Several students expressed a want for seminars which address the topic of food insecurity, both to help reduce stigma and for direction on nutritious, low-cost food choices and meal planning. Other students expressed the need for help in finding a job and navigating the process of finding work at UNT, or that they would benefit from UNT removing the cap on the number of hours that students could work. Another consistent suggestion was to have food drives which are embraced in an entertaining manner. Student suggestions included a "canstruction" event similar to years past, as well as having graduate/undergraduate student competitions within departments or student organizations to bring in donations for the UNT Food Pantry. A reduced-price meal plan option was suggested by several students, primarily those who fell into the very low food secure category of the U.S. Food Security Survey. When students talked about the creation of this option, they reflected on their past, and how they qualified for free- or reduced-price lunches in K-12. One student suggested determining qualification for the reduced-price meal plans according to their FAFSA scores, stating that the information was already in the system and it would be easy to implement (see below for discussion at the national level). Another type of suggestion was directed at pricing and hours of the eateries in the University Union. Several students stated that the Union's pricing was too expensive. One student reflected on how she wanted to buy grapes, but was not willing to pay over

$2.50 for a small cup of fruit. Another student suggested to add a UNT bus route to the grocery store on Saturdays. There is an area where several grocery stores are close together, and this infrastructural change could help to increase access for students on campus without transportation.

6.2.4   *Solutions Students Would Not Use*

Most participants could not think of university solutions they would be unwilling to use to help alleviate their food insecurity. Some students said that if programs needed more personal information or were seen as an unfair exchange, they would not use those solutions. Others stated they would not use solutions that required too much of their own time or that made them feel judged.

6.3   Student-Suggested Solutions Beyond UNT

Participants were asked to think about solutions beyond UNT that would be the most helpful for their situation. The strongest response (40%) was that an increase to their income would help them the most. Many stated that once they graduate and have a degree, they expect to find a job which will offer this increase to their income. Getting a second job was also mentioned (22%) as a way to increase income. Finding less expensive housing as a solution to food insecurity was mentioned by 19.5 percent of participants. Many students reflected on the struggle to find affordable housing close to campus. Interestingly, the solutions they stated did not include assistance. They talked about ways to increase their income and reduce their expenses.

It is noteworthy to discuss non-UNT food pantries and free lunches in this section. Only a few participants mentioned non-UNT food pantries or free lunches during any part of the interview, and no participants mentioned these programs as potential solutions beyond UNT. There are two nearby church-based student organizations that offer weekly free lunches and a weekly church food pantry. These organizations are on the UNT campus, but are not formally part of the UNT organizational structure. When asked directly about whether or not they had ever attended one of these free lunches or the church food pantry, 22 percent of participants said yes to one free lunch spot, 31 percent said yes to the second free lunch spot, and 28 percent said yes to the church food pantry. Even with a quarter to one-third of the participants knowing about these services, students did not discuss them or other local community-based soup kitchens as possibilities when asked about other solutions. This further suggests that UNT students prefer to rely on UNT programs for solutions to food insecurity and hunger rather than on outside resources.

6.4   NATIONWIDE CONFERENCES, PROGRAMS, INTERVENTIONS, AND POLICY

The nation is talking about food insecurity among college students—the federal government, researchers, university administrators, faculty, students, as well as non-profit organizations. In this section, I briefly discuss some of the interventions and solutions that are being implemented at colleges and universities throughout the U.S. and guide the reader to additional information when possible.

6.4.1   *The Hope Center for College, Community, and Justice*

The Hope Center for College, Community, and Justice, a non-profit action research center founded by Sara Goldrick-Rab, is at the forefront of the national discussion about #RealCollege students. The Center focuses on the complexities of challenges that impact college students' lives, particularly food and housing security. The Center's team works on research, evidence-based recommendations for influencing institutional practices and policies, and a national convening. #RealCollege: A National Convening on College Food & Housing Insecurity is a conference that brings together leaders working to reduce the burden of food and housing insecurity on students. The speaker list varies from year to year, but typically includes university administrators, politicians, founders of non-profits, top researchers, and experts who run workshops on topics from implementing interventions to effective lobbying to administrators and policymakers. I was invited to participate in a research workshop at the 2017 #RealCollege convening. See the Hope Center website (https://hope4college.com/) for additional information on their mission and projects.

6.4.2   *The GOA Report and Introduced Legislation*

As noted in Chap. 1, the U.S. Government Accountability Office (GAO) published a report to Congress in December 2018 that reviewed food insecurity among college students. The federal government has a substantial investment in higher education, and if students are not graduating because of issues with food insecurity, that investment is being wasted. The report examines "(1) what is known about the extent of food insecurity among college students and their use of SNAP; (2) how selected colleges are addressing student food insecurity; and (3) the extent to which federal programs assist students experiencing food insecurity" (GAO 2018, X). The report highlights that in 2016 almost two million at-risk students did not receive SNAP benefits for which they were potentially eligible. The GOA Report recommends that the USDA Food and Nutrition Service (FNS) "(1) improve student eligibility information [about SNAP] on its website and (2) share information on state SNAP agencies' approaches to help eligible students" (GAO 2018, X).

One major issue with students and SNAP benefits is that both university officials and students are unfamiliar with the student eligibility rules. In the 2014 UNT pilot study, students did not talk about social services—not about using them nor as potential solutions. For this reason, students in the 2017 UNT research were asked a series of questions about social services, including their knowledge of social services, their ideas about who services are for, and whether or not they would apply for services. Over 75 percent of participants had a general knowledge about social services. However, there was general confusion and frustration about the application and eligibility requirements. Many students had heard that they need to work at least 20 hours per week to be approved; however, it was unclear whether students needed to be in school full-time in addition to the work requirement. Other students stated that it was not easy to maintain 20 hours per week with entry-level, low-paying jobs. Corbin, a 19-year-old African-American freshman who lives on campus, noted: *When you're a student, you have to work 20 hours a week. I ended up losing my SNAP benefits because I wasn't able to work enough. My boss couldn't get my hours up over like 13 hours. So, the food stamps place was like well sorry, you know, and they just cut it off and I was like 'well, cool, great.'* Another student told a story of being on the phone with the SNAP office for an hour, being told she would need to fax in documents, and if the information was not received within two weeks, the case would close, and she would have to start over. Other students commented on the ways in which one could lose benefits. For example, they understood that they did not qualify for SNAP if they lived in the dorms. Additionally, if they received too much money in disability or social security, their benefits may be adjusted, or they may not qualify anymore. Especially of concern to students was the issue of receiving too much aid. If they received too much financial aid or other loans/money to pay for school, they understood that their benefits may be adjusted, or they may not qualify anymore. A few students also pointed out that when that threshold of disqualification is crossed, the struggle will increase for a period of time until one can find a way to make more money or save money elsewhere.

UNT participants were also asked who they felt social services serve. All of the students responded with "those in need," but most did not include themselves in that category. Most participants stated that they believed services were for families. Andie, a 21-year-old Mexican-American senior, said: *I guess I just learned or assumed it was a family-need based thing. I guess it always felt like something a parent would do to help their children. So now I guess I don't really know very much about these programs. I have never really looked into it or anything.*

Finally, students were asked whether they would ever apply for social services. Overall, 72 percent of participants said they would apply for SNAP benefits and 28 percent said they would not apply. For those who would apply, the majority specified that they would apply if they truly felt that they needed that level of help. A few others also said that the only way that they would apply for services is if they believed that their situation was longer than temporary. Some students said that they would apply if there was someone who could help them walk through the process. There was some inquiry about whether a person could be in that role on the UNT campus, someone who could specifically help students to navigate through the social service system. For those who would not apply, the majority said they did not want the government in their business or because of the stigma associated with using social services. Kendra, a 20-year-old African-American junior who lived on campus, said: *I don't want to be that person who's, I guess, lazy and using another worker's hard-earned money. I don't want to be perceived as sitting down on the couch doing nothing.*

Interestingly, even though UNT students were asked a series of questions about social services, when pressed about solutions beyond the university later in the interview, most did not mention applying for social services. They relied primarily on the university for assistance. However, the majority of students who did discuss SNAP benefits as a solution also had prior experiences with SNAP benefits as children.

In July 2019, a new bill called Closing the College Hunger Gap was introduced by Senator Chris Murphy of Connecticut and Representatives Jahana Hayes of Connecticut and Marcia Fudge of Ohio. The bill is a response to the 2018 GOA Report and designed to curtail the critics who suggest there is not enough reliable data to enact federal level solutions. The bill calls for requiring the collection of food and housing insecurity data among college students so that standardized data is collected annually across the nation. The questions would be added to the National Postsecondary Student Aid Study, which is already administered to college students. The bill would also require that students are notified of their food stamp eligibility when they apply for federal financial aid (Harris 2019).

6.4.3   Increase Access to Social Services

Increasing student access to social services is a growing priority across the nation and one that has evidence of improving academic success. As noted above, the 2018 GOA Report recommends improving informational resources of student eligibility for SNAP at the federal and state levels. UNT currently has a representative from the local SNAP office who comes to campus once per month. The Dean of Students tables information about the upcoming event at the library mall for several days prior in order to increase awareness.

One non-profit organization, Single Stop, goes further. Single Stop utilizes technology and a vast network of government and community-based resources to connect students to wrap-around services at a single stop location on campus. The program was founded in 2001 and started partnering with colleges in 2009. Single Stop supports colleges in connecting students with a wide range of benefits and services. They help students understand what they are eligible for and how to apply for those services. The goal is to eliminate non-academic barriers to academic success so students can make it to the next year and successfully graduate. Their goal is to provide a "holistic support network" to connect students with "comprehensive resources" that "alleviate barriers" to success. Evaluation studies by RAND Corporation and Metis Associates show that students who used Single Stop while in college were more successful than their peers who did not use Single Stop, particularly increased first-time-in-college retention, higher pass rates, higher GPAs, and higher graduation rates (Daugherty et al. 2016; Zhu et al. 2018). More information on Single Stop can be found here: https://singlestopusa.org/#home-page.

The Center for Law and Policy (CLASP) has created a free webinar that explains the basics of SNAP and how university campuses can accept Electronic Benefits Transfer (EBT) at campus eateries and stores. (see

https://www.youtube.com/watch?v=00nFZCItZhU&featur
e=youtu.be).

The Hope Center for College, Community, and Justice and CLASP call for an expansion of the Federal National School Lunch Program to university students. Those who are already Pell Grant recipients could qualify for meal assistance to reduce administrative overhead (Goldrick-Rab et al. 2016; Blumenthal and Chu 2018).

6.4.4   University Meal Donations

Universities across the country provide meal swipe donation programs to alleviate food insecurity on campus. One national program is Swipe Out Hunger, which was founded in 2010 by a group of friends at the University of California Los Angeles. Swipe Out Hunger has partnered with over 80 universities and has served 1.7 million nutritious meals as of July 2019. Not only does the organization partner with universities to establish meal swipe donation programs, but it also provides marketing, education, coaching, and evaluation. For more information, see their website: https://www.swipehunger.org/partnerwithus/#why-partner.

Another organization, founded at New York University, is Share Meals. Share Meals has a digital platform that allows students to connect with each other in real-time to share meal swipes and post when extra food is available from club events. The organization has additional initiatives, such as Packathon, that reallocates extra club funding to make sandwiches for fellow students, and Open Kitchen, which is a series of cooking classes and demonstrations. For more information, see their website: https://sharemeals.org/.

6.4.5   Meal Vouchers and Food Scholarships

Other existing university-driven solutions include meal vouchers and food scholarships, such as those highlighted in the evaluation work by the Hope Center for College, Community, and Justice at the beginning of this chapter. Bunker Hill Community College partners with Single Stop and has a College Hunger Team. In 2017, the Team started a pilot program with 110 students who were identified as food insecure. The program provides a $25/week meal voucher to be used via electronic debit card at any of the college's foodservice venues. Houston Community College partners with the local food bank to distribute food scholarships to students. In 2017, the college started piloting a program to bring food scholarships to students. Recipients have some choice in the food that is received, and much of it is fresh fruits and vegetables, frozen meat, and other nutritious items (Goldrick-Rab et al. 2018a).

6.4.6   Emergency Loans and Aid

Some universities are tackling the financial crisis head-on, including UNT, by providing financial relief programs such as short-term, interest-free loans, emergency scholarships, book loan programs, and free tax-preparation services (Broton and Goldrick-Rab 2018). The Hope Center for College, Community, and Justice offers a guide for faculty to set up their own emergency aid program. One such program, called FAST (Faculty and Students Together), has provided funding to faculty at 13 different colleges. The idea of the FAST program is that faculty often knows students very well and often know when they are struggling. A faculty emergency aid fund is meant to cut out the cumbersome application process of funds provided through formal university channels. It is meant to be quick small amounts of cash given directly to students for specific financial needs. For more information on general guidelines, see https://hope4college.com/wp-content/uploads/2019/05/Emergency-Student-Aid-Brief.pdf. For more information on the FAST fund, see http://www.thefastfund.org/.

6.4.7   Increased Skills Training

Universities and programs are also paying more attention to increasing skills training for college students. Watson et al. (2017) conducted research at the University of California Los Angeles on the topics of food insecurity and food literacy. Participants expressed frustration with knowing which foods are nutritious, but having limited resources and knowledge of how to adequately prepare that type of food. They wanted the university to provide food education and training, particularly regarding food budgeting and preparing quick nutritious meals. As mentioned above, the Share Meals program offers to partner with colleges to start Open Kitchen, which is a series of cooking classes and demonstrations (see also Martinez et al. 2016).

All UNT students have access to a dietitian, who is available for appointments. The UNT Dietitian website has nutritional resources for students that include suggestions for apartments and residence halls. See https://studentaffairs.unt.edu/student-health-and-wellness-center/services/dietitian.

6.4.8   *Increased Visibility*

Amarillo College in the panhandle of Texas is taking a different approach. The community college offers many programs that can be found at other universities, such as a food pantry, fast emergency funds, social workers, legal aid, mental health counseling, a low-cost daycare, transportation services, and so forth. It is drawing national attention for its focus on addressing the effects of poverty, holistically and visibly. The Advocacy and Resource Center (ARC) is the center of the college's poverty work and functions as a one-stop center to help students with university, federal, state, and community-based resources. It is located on the first floor of the student commons building and is surrounded by glass. The idea is that making the center visible and accessible to all students helps destigmatize going to the food pantry and creates a culture where faculty, staff, and students recognize that students in poverty are just one crisis away from dropping out (Lowery-Hart et al. 2017; Bombardieri 2018). Goldrick-Rab et al. (2018b), in their report on campus food pantries, point out the debate on the value of privacy versus an open concept for encouraging students to utilize campus pantries and resources. Some suggest that privacy is better for the students' self-esteem. Others suggest that having resources in visible, open areas helps normalize poverty and resources (Goldrick-Rab et al. 2018b). UNT participants seem to value a broader conversation about poverty and food insecurity to reduce stigma across campus, but would like a relatively discrete food pantry location to reduce stigma and shame. Future research would show if this sentiment changes as the conversation broadens on the UNT campus.

NOTE

1. The Dean of Students office does give out cafeteria meal vouchers to students in crisis on a case-by-case basis. However, no UNT participants mentioned these vouchers so they were not included in the UNT analysis.

REFERENCES

Blumenthal, Susan, and Christina Chu. 2018. Food Insecurity on College Campuses: A Recipe for Action, April 4. https://www.clasp.org/press-room/news-clips/food-insecurity-college-campuses. Accessed 15 June 2019.

Bombardieri, Marcella. 2018. Colleges Are No Match for American Poverty. *The Atlantic*, May. https://www.theatlantic.com/education/archive/2018/05/college-poor-students/560972/. Accessed 4 Dec 2018.

Broton, Katharine M., and Clare L. Cady, eds. 2020. *Food Insecurity on Campus: Action and Intervention*. Baltimore, MD: Johns Hopkins University Press.

Broton, Katharine, and Sara Goldrick-Rab. 2018. Going Without: An Exploration of Food and Housing Insecurity Among Undergraduates. *Educational Researcher* 47 (2): 121–133. https://doi.org/10.3102/0013189x17741303.

Butler, Mary Odell. 2015. *Evaluation: A Cultural Systems Approach*. London: Routledge.

Daugherty, Lindsay, William R. Johnston, and Tiffany Tsai. 2016. Connecting College Students to Alternative Sources of Support: The Single Stop Community College Initiative and Postsecondary Outcomes. https://www.singlestopusa.org/wp-content/uploads/2016/11/RAND-Report_Executive-Summary-1.pdf.

Goldrick-Rab, Sara, Katharine Broton, and Emily Brunjes Colo. 2016. Expanding the National School Lunch Program to Higher Education. Report. https://hope4college.com/wp-content/uploads/2018/09/Wisconsin-HOPE-Expand-Lunch_Program.pdf. Accessed 20 July 2019.

Goldrick-Rab, Sara, Katharine M. Broton, and Daphne C. Hernandez. 2018a. *Addressing Basic Needs Security in Higher Education: An Introduction to Three Evaluations of Supports for Food and Housing at Community College*. Report. https://hope4college.com/wp-content/uploads/2018/09/Addressing-Basic-Needs-Security-in-Higher-Education.pdf. Accessed 1 June 2019.

Goldrick-Rab, Sara, Clare Cady, and Vanessa Coca. 2018b. *Campus Food Pantries: Insights from a National Survey*. Report, September. https://hope4college.com/campus-food-pantries-insights-from-a-national-survey/. Accessed 11 Nov 2018.

Goldrick-Rab, Sara, Jed Richardson, and Peter Kinsley. 2018c. *Guide to Assessing Basic Needs Insecurity in Higher Education*. Report, July. https://hope4college.com/wp-content/uploads/2018/09/Basic-Needs-Insecurity-College-Students.pdf. Accessed 8 Feb 2019.

Government Accountability Office (GAO). 2018. *Better Information Could Help Eligible College Students Access Federal Food Assistance Benefits*. Report. U.S. Government Accountability Office, December. https://www.gao.gov/assets/700/696254.pdf. Accessed 18 May 2019.

Harris, Adam. 2019. Many College Students Are Too Poor to Eat. *The Atlantic*, July 11. https://www.theatlantic.com/education/archive/2019/07/lawmakers-introduce-bill-address-campus-hunger/593704/. Accessed 28 July 2019.

Lowery-Hart, Russell, Cara Crowley, and Jordan Herrera. 2017. No Excuses: A Systemic Approach to Student Poverty. *Diversity & Democracy* 20 (4 Fall). https://www.aacu.org/diversitydemocracy/2017/fall/lowery-hart.

Martinez, Suzanna, E. Brown, and L. Ritchie. 2016. What Factors Increase Risk for Food Insecurity Among College Students? *Journal of Nutrition Education and Behavior* 48 (7): S4. https://doi.org/10.1016/j.jneb.2016.04.017.

Watson, Tyler D., Hannah Malan, Deborah Glik, and Suzanna M. Martinez. 2017. College Students Identify University Support for Basic Needs and Life Skills as Key Ingredient in Addressing Food Insecurity on Campus. *California Agriculture* 71 (3): 130–138. https://doi.org/10.3733/ca.2017a0023.

Zhu, Jing, Susanne Harnett, and Michael Scuello. 2018. Single Stop Final Impact and Implementation Report, September. https://www.singlestopusa.org/wp-content/uploads/2019/04/Single-Stop-Final-Impact-and-Implementation-Study-final.pdf. Accessed 27 July 2019.

CHAPTER 7

Conclusions

Abstract This chapter functions as the book's conclusion. I begin by revisiting the literature on food insecurity among college students, followed by an emphasis on the root of food insecurity among college students—that college is unaffordable for low-income students, financial aid does not adequately cover the needed expenses, and students are willing to sacrifice basic needs in order to get a college degree. Next, I discuss the national awareness of the issues, including legislation, multi-sited prevalence studies, and the importance of understanding the local context of each university. I draw together themes from all of the chapters and emphasize the important, complementary contribution of this qualitative study to the existing studies. The closing section reexamines the best ways to alleviate the food insecurity and hunger sacrifices UNT students are willing to make for their degree. Finally, I conclude with an update on what has been happening at UNT since data collection for this research.

Keywords Food insecurity • Follow up

Prevalence studies show that an average of 44 percent of students has experienced food insecurity while attending college (Goldrick-Rab et al. 2019). When compared to the national average of 11.8 percent (data from 2017), it becomes clear that college students are disproportionally food insecure. They even have a higher rate of food insecurity than every other comparison group, including households with children headed by a single woman (30.3%) and households that are below 185 percent of the poverty threshold (30.8%) (USDA 2018). Yet, questions remain about how college students experience food insecurity differently than the general population.

College is increasingly more expensive than for previous generations (Goldrick-Rab 2016). The student population is changing to include more students who are already considered vulnerable populations, such as older students, first-generation, low-income, working, more diverse, and those with family obligations to balance. These students often do not have enough financial resources to cover the rising costs of education. Federal financial aid helps, such as the Pell Grant. Federal loans help. University scholarships and grants help. However, oftentimes, even with all of these financial resources combined, it is still not enough to cover the expenses. Students and their families are trying to make up the difference. Nationally, 68 percent of food insecure students work at least part-time. At UNT, 72 percent of participants in the research study work. Many students still fall financially short.

Students are willing to sacrifice. With all of the struggles—the hunger, the poor nutrition, the lack of energy, the difficulty concentrating, the stress, depression and anxiety, the juggling of work and class time—they are still motivated to stay in college. They acknowledged that staying in school despite food insecurity and other stressors takes priority over hunger and health. They are motivated by the knowledge that a college degree is a step toward financial security, something some students have never had.

Fortunately, for college students across the country, the nation is paying attention. Research at the national and local levels is rapidly increasing. There was only a handful of research publications about food insecurity among college students when I published the pilot study in 2017. Now there are dozens of publications each year. In 2017, legislation was introduced to Congress to modify and expand SNAP eligibility for college students (College Student Hunger Act of 2017 and the Foster and Homeless Youth Food Security Act of 2017). Neither of these bills have moved out of the House of Representatives; however; in 2018, the Government Office of Accountability published a report to Congress that reviewed the issue of food insecurity among college students. The report examined what is known about food insecurity on college campuses, what colleges are doing to address the issue locally, and how students use federal resources like SNAP benefits. In response, a new billed was introduced in

2019 called Closing the College Hunger Gap. This new bill calls for routine data collection to understand the issue nationwide, as well as increased information about existing federal assistance programs. It is important for scholars to write policy briefs and inform lawmakers of recommended solutions.

Continued research is important. At the national level, longitudinal multi-university studies help to explain the yearly prevalence of food insecurity among college students. They also help find patterns in the characteristics of students, risk factors, and the experiences of food insecurity across universities. These studies provide a broad scope of the similarities and complexities that exist among similar universities, as well as among universities that are significantly different. For example, if community colleges and private universities share patterns in how students experience food insecurity, then that could provide information on solutions that may apply across universities. If female African-American students have the highest rates of food insecurity across all studies, then that is valuable information about a high-risk group that should be given extra attention.

At the local level, research is needed to understand the specific context of a university. Two- and four-year colleges and universities are as different as their towns, cities, states, and regions of the U.S. They have different missions, different resources, different stakeholders, and different students. The voices of students should be heard within the context of their specific colleges. Local experiences may have similarities and patterns as those across the nation, but the students' specific experiences, their history, their stories, their strategies, and so forth will all be shaped by the local context of their university.

The goal of all of this research though is not only to understand the problem of food insecurity among college students, but also to bring awareness of the issue at a large enough scale, with excellent data, to develop solutions. Universities throughout the U.S. have departments or divisions similar to the UNT Dean of Students. These departments are dedicated to supporting students and serving as an advocate for those who need assistance with managing a crisis, looking for the right resources, or assisting in complex personal and academic affairs. Resolving the issue of hunger and food insecurity for some students is part of that mission in order to help students achieve their personal and academic goals. Food insecurity is associated with poor nutrition, physical health consequences, stress, depression, lack of concentration, poor sleep habits, and anxiety. Students who experience some or all of the above symptoms are more likely to experience decreased academic success. University administrators concerned with graduation and retention rates should understand that food insecurity is a threat and barrier to academic success.

As discussed in Chap. 6: Solutions, universities across the country are implementing programmatic solutions, many of which are guided by research and/or are being evaluated to measure their success. As noted by Broton and Cady (2020), there is no one solution to solving the issue of food insecurity among college students. Solutions should be multifaceted. Some students might need short-term solutions like cafeteria meal vouchers for a month until they receive a new paycheck. Some students might need items from a food pantry that can be easily heated and eaten in a dorm room. Some students might need an emergency loan to repair a car. Some students might need a more long-term solution like secure housing or SNAP benefits because they have dependents to support. Colleges have students with diverse needs who will benefit from a variety of programs that are tailored to meet those needs. These programs should be partnered with solutions at the national, state, and local community levels as well.

7.1   At the University of North Texas

This qualitative research attempts to capture the richness of the UNT students' experiences of food insecurity while attending college. I give voice to their perspectives, their experiences, and their everyday practices of being food insecure and hungry while trying to finish their degrees. The significance is in the detail, their words, their passions, their pain, their struggles, their coping, and their motivation and perseverance to finish. The reasons that universities do the work to help their students succeed are in the pages of this manuscript. There is no unified experience of food insecurity. There are patterns, yes, but every student in this study had a story to tell of how they got to this point, how they felt, what they did to cope, and how the food pantry helped. There are tipping points, meal plans without weekends, and transportation issues. There are coping strategies to make food stretch, sleeping through hunger, drinking water, and distraction. Some had childhood experiences that seem to give them a stronger sense of resolve about their situation.

Stigma, shame, and embarrassment are pervasive themes throughout the students' experiences. There is shame about being food insecure in college, being food insecure as children, federal social services, student perceptions, the food pantry, and talking about their situation. Only 41 percent of participants said they have someone to talk to about food insecurity; however, 94 percent said they think a broader conversation about food insecurity coming from the university would be beneficial for reducing stigma and increasing knowledge of resources. Research shows that social support and communal meals may decrease some of the negative impacts of food insecurity (Dirks and Carter 1980; Martin et al. 2004; Higashi et al. 2017; Watson et al. 2017; Allen and Alleman 2019).

UNT students associate food insecurity with poor nutrition, poor physical health, poor mental health, and decreased academic performance. They understand that cheap food is highly processed and low in nutritional value. They understand the connection between nutrient-poor food, lack of energy, lack of concentration, and lower academic performance. They also understand the relationship between worry and stress about finances and food with depression, anxiety, and lower academic performance. They talked about missing class to work extra shifts and not buying books because they need to eat. Yet despite all of these struggles, they had strong feelings about being motivated to graduate. They understand food insecurity in college to be temporary.

In terms of solutions, UNT food insecure students would benefit from a combination of increased knowledge and access to federal food assistance programs, local community resources, and additional university solutions. UNT students do not often think about potential solutions beyond the university. They know they could stop taking classes, work more hours, and probably not be food insecure. They look for ways to increase their income and decrease their expenses. Therefore, most do not think of themselves as needing (or worthy of) federal or state assistance and prefer to work and make it on their own, with some assistance from the university. For this reason, UNT students would benefit from more information coming directly from the university about outside resources, such as SNAP, community lunches, and other benefits/resources for which they may qualify. Because stigma and shame are issues that students spoke about, discretion needs to be considered with all solutions. Students want a broader conversation about food insecurity at UNT to decrease stigma; but at the same time, when information and resources are directed at them personally (like going to the food pantry or signing up for assistance), they prefer discretion and privacy.

One of the biggest issues that all UNT food insecure students have is lack of time. Students have a fair amount of knowledge about what they should be doing to eat healthy. What they do not have are time and resources. Students would benefit from additional education on low-cost, nutrient-dense, and easy to prepare food.

7.2 UNT Happenings Post Research

Data from this research was shared with the Dean of Students in December 2017, and much has happened at UNT since that time. The word is spreading about the UNT Food Pantry. Backing up to its opening in January 2015, by the end of that academic year, it had 436 client visits. By the time we started the research project in February 2017, it had 1754 client visits. By the end of July 2019, it had 6677 client visits in total (Fig. 7.1).

Great things are happening at the UNT Food Pantry too. The Dean of Students is working with the North Texas Food Bank to become a monthly stop for the North Texas Food Bank Mobile Pantry. This mobile food pantry will provide an accessible and convenient source for fresh fruits and vegetables on campus. This resource should be available by the fall 2019 semester. The UNT Community Garden has several plots that are dedicated for donations to the UNT Food Pantry. The main UNT Food Pantry is moving out of the University Union. It will be located on the ground floor of a university dorm in a new space dedicated to "Suit Up, Fuel Up, and Cap Up," a three-program initiative that will promote student success and career readiness to those in need. Suit Up is a program to

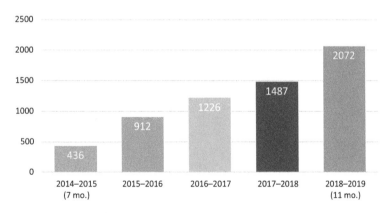

Fig. 7.1 Number of pantry clients per year

provide students with professional clothing for successful internships and interviews. The space will provide fitting rooms and a permanent location for the program to loan professional clothes year-round. Cap Up is also called the Mean Green Gown for Grads and provides free cap and gown rentals for graduating seniors in need. Fuel Up refers to the UNT Food Pantry. The new space will be bigger and will offer refrigerated and frozen items, such as fresh fruits, vegetables, dairy, and possibly meat. The Dean of Students is building partnerships with community food banks to ensure steady and reliable food donations. They are working with the UNT dietitian to strategize how food will be offered in the new space. They understand that students need quick, healthy, easy to prepare foods. One idea is to offer bagged meals with recipe cards that students can pick up and readily have all the items they need for preparing that meal. There would be meals for students with kitchens and meals for students living in dorms. The Dean of Students is restructuring the food pantry team to add a volunteer Student Board of Directors, as well as restructuring the pantry volunteer opportunities. Finally, the Dean of Students is re-evaluating the pantry hours and staffing options as they prepare for their move to the new space.

In 2018, UNT started a broader conversation on campus about food insecurity. The campus participated in Hunger and Homelessness Awareness Week, which is sponsored by the National Coalition for the Homeless and the National Student Campaign Against Hunger and Homelessness. The awareness week is an annual program that takes place around the nation to raise awareness about the problems of hunger and homelessness. Although the week is not exclusively about college students, some of the UNT activities were designed to raise awareness about college food insecurity and bring in donations for the UNT Food Pantry. UNT is currently planning the 2019 Hunger and Homelessness Awareness Week activities.

REFERENCES

Allen, Cara Cliburn, and Nathan F. Alleman. 2019. A Private Struggle at a Private Institution: Effects of Student Hunger on Social and Academic Experiences. *Journal of College Student Development* 60 (1): 52–69. doi:10.1353/csd.2019.0003.

Broton, Katharine M., and Clare L. Cady, eds. 2020. *Food Insecurity on Campus: Action and Intervention.* Baltimore, MD: Johns Hopkins University Press.

Dirks, Robert, and James P. Carter. 1980. Social Responses During Severe Food Shortages and Famine. *Current Anthropology* 21 (1): 21–44. https://doi.org/10.1016/b978-0-08-027998-5.50017-9.

Goldrick-Rab, Sara. 2016. *Paying the Price: College Costs, Financial Aid, and the Betrayal of the American Dream.* Chicago, IL: University of Chicago Press.

Goldrick-Rab, Sara, Christine Baker-Smith, Vanessa Coca, Elizabeth Looker, and Tiffani Williams. 2019. *College and University Basic Needs Insecurity: A National #RealCollege Survey Report.* Report, April. https://hope4college.com/wp-content/uploads/2019/04/HOPE_realcollege_National_report_digital.pdf. Accessed 18 May 2019.

Higashi, Robin T., Simon Craddock Lee, Carla Pezzia, Lisa Quirk, Tammy Leonard, and Sandi L. Pruitt. 2017. Family and Social Context Contributes to the Interplay of Economic Insecurity, Food Insecurity, and Health. *Annals of Anthropological Practice* 41 (2): 67–77. https://doi.org/10.1111/napa.12114.

Martin, Katie S., Beatrice L. Rogers, John T. Cook, and Hugh M. Joseph. 2004. Social Capital Is Associated with Decreased Risk of Hunger. *Social Science & Medicine* 58 (12): 2645–2654. https://doi.org/10.1016/j.socscimed.2003.09.026.

US Department of Agriculture Economic Research Service. 2018. *Food Security in the U.S. Key Statistics & Graphics.* https://www.ers.usda.gov/topics/food-nutrition-assistance/food-security-in-the-us/key-statistics-graphics/. Accessed 8 Sep 2018.

Watson, Tyler D., Hannah Malan, Deborah Glik, and Suzanna M. Martinez. 2017. College Students Identify University Support for Basic Needs and Life Skills as Key Ingredient in Addressing Food Insecurity on Campus. *California Agriculture* 71 (3): 130–138. https://doi.org/10.3733/ca.2017a0023.

Index[1]

[1] Note: Page numbers followed by 'n' refer to notes.